UPSET IS
OPTIONAL

PRAISE FOR *Upset is Optional*

The great healers of human history have all had a special gift for reconnecting individuals to the healing power already dwelling within themselves. And it was this special gift that Bob Duggan's life of service brought to our times. (Like Francis of Assisi, Bob believed "we have been called to heal wounds, to unite what has fallen apart, and to bring home those who have lost their way.")

With compelling stories and an urgent relevance for our times, Karen Howard has done a masterful job of bringing Bob's powerful lessons of hope and healing to an even broader audience.

> —**Governor Martin O'Malley,**
> **Governor of Maryland [2007–2015]**

Upset is Optional is a no-nonsense roadmap to living your best life. For anyone seeking sustainable change in their daily lives, the principles within these pages are the precise tools to accomplish those goals.

> —**Naomi Whittel, CEO, Naomi Whittel Brands,**
> ***New York Times* best-selling author of**
> ***Glow15: A Science-Based Plan to Lose Weight,***
> ***Revitalize Your Skin, and Invigorate Your Life***

"What would your life be like if you had access to a trusted, credible, and experienced friend to act as a guide in understanding the interconnectedness between our challenges in life and the opportunity for personal growth and a greater, more "in the flow" experience on our path? Well, I have been blessed with such a friend in Karen Howard. And I am thrilled that in this book, she provides the valuable tools and insight designed to align your inner rhythm and higher awareness with one major goal—to make your life feel more purposeful, fulfilling, and joyful.

—Michael Murray, ND
Author of more than thirty books
with over 6-million copies sold

UPSET IS OPTIONAL

OPTIONAL

Say Goodbye to Unnecessary Suffering

KAREN HOWARD

I dedicate this book to Sophia and Max.
Honor your past and be true to your future.

ACKNOWLEDGMENTS

I want to thank my publishing team, Tanya Brockett and Kathy Kaye, for giving me the courage, support, and amazing advice I needed to get this book onto the shelves and into the hands of the people it will serve. Their expertise enabled me to complete this part of my journey and point me to new horizons.

I would never have attained this goal without the support of an incredible group of teachers and friends at Bob's beloved Tai Sophia. Susan Duggan, you have held my hand through more "firsts" than I ever could have imagined, and guided me through the fires that brought me to a renewed place of intention. To Anne Huyler Baker, Dianne Connelly, and Jade Connelly Duggan, my gratitude for your guidance and patience is deep.

Terri Deerr, David Matteson, Debbie Daniels, Mimi Welch, Kimberly Dorsey Bronow, Amy Summers, Devra Kudeviz, and Sandy Howard enriched this journey with your wisdom, guidance, and love. I would travel to the end of the world with you, again.

Paul Abowd and Joe Tasto, you put your faith in a process and stood by this project with enormous patience and award-worthy insight.

And to my fellow students, thank you for sharing your teaching stories and for teaching your children how to be a healing presence in the world. That is what these words on the page are all about.

CONTENTS

PART III

**Do not abdicate your power in the time
you have on Earth. Engineer your day to
effectively use the gifts you've been given.**

Preface

In just a few days, I will mark the death of my friend and mentor Bob Duggan. I remember exactly where I was, each word of the phone call, the horrible constriction of my chest, and the numbness in my arms. Even in his passing, he was able to call me into my body, completely aware of how my emotion impacted my breathing or lack thereof. I quickly decided I wanted to write this book and share his gifts. It's taken me three years to truly commit my fingers to the keyboard.

Bob was a native of New York City. Raised Catholic, he entered the priesthood at a young age. A rising star, he quickly made his way to a post at the Vatican. Among his other duties there, he led a conversation designed to create dialogue between members of the clergy and laypeople. It worked. It was there he met Dianne Connelly, the woman he married after he left the church. It was not the usual way of being, but Bob's mentor was historian and scholar, Ivan Illich. Illich taught him to question certitudes, explaining everything is "based on made-up human assumptions." His choices landed him on a very early episode of the Phil Donahue show that highlighted the reasons young priests were leaving the church.

It was in the late sixties when Bob began a forty-four-year journey as an acupuncturist, healer, and transformative force of nature. He and Dianne established a home base in New York, traveled to Asia, and found their way to England. There, they met and were treated by J. R. Worsley, the British acupuncturist credited with bringing traditional, five element acupuncture from China to the West. They opened their acupuncture clinic at a time when it was illegal to practice in most states. They also founded one of the first accredited acupuncture schools in the United States.

In the early nineties, he started Penn North, a nonprofit community center in the drug-plagued neighborhood of Baltimore City. Penn North still uses acupuncture 'pins,' the use of needles being relegated to drugs, to support addiction recovery. He testified at the White House Commission on Complementary and Alternative Medicine, at the National Institutes of Health, and before the Senate Committee on Health, Education, Labor, and Pensions. He also advised the presidential campaign of Maryland Governor Martin O'Malley. *Common Sense for the Healing Arts: Essays by Bob Duggan* was published in 2003. This book called people to realize possibility in their lives and their duty to serve those around them and the generations to come. Bob's 2009 TED Talk was entitled "Evolving as Leaders." His last book in

2012, *Breaking the Iron Triangle*, details the false dilemma that cost, quality, and access are key to solving our current healthcare crisis. His message consistently stated that 1.2 trillion of the country's annual healthcare expenditures could be avoided if individuals made common lifestyle changes.

When I met Bob in 2003, he quickly transformed my worldview of our disease-driven healthcare system and fueled my life's passion for affecting change. I became a student at his beloved Tai (The Acupuncture Institute) Sophia (School of Philosophy and Healing in Action) Institute.

Renowned for its acupuncture program, I enrolled in its sister program (the Applied Healing Arts program), beginning an adventure that I will travel for my lifetime. The program allowed students to explore the roots of five-element acupuncture. Instead of using needles, we ventured to be a healing presence in the world through words and actions. I fell in love with philosophy and immersed myself in a language unique to the program and incredibly foreign to the ears of family and friends. I still call upon those teachings.

After thirty-six years, Bob left Tai Sophia with the title President Emeritus. Everything changes with time. Different does not always mean better. Originally a champion for accreditation and licensure, he came to regret the reductionist impact these norms have on empowering individuals and their practitioners to know their own bodies and symptoms. Tai Sophia was remarkable because Bob was training a wellness workforce, not teaching practitioners how to alleviate symptoms. The school's new intention to transition to a university pitted founding philosophies against a newly-articulated dream of progress. Its current incarnation as the Maryland University of Integrative Health only resembles the original Tai Sophia. This gave Bob new incentive to hone his teaching for the sake of accessibility.

He created a unique apprentice program to teach the practices in this book, instilling in us that we would know we were successful when we felt the impact of the practice in our bodies. He demanded that we take it into the world and give it away every day, in our homes, at work, or on a stage to friends, family, and clients. He was fierce in his belief that we only have this short time on Earth. He asked, "Who are we to squander our precious gifts?" His voice is what inspired me to teach the practices to you.

Introduction

I n this book, I ask you to practice. It's not an uncommon request. As children, we were always being pushed to practice. If you played an instrument, a sport, or even video games, you practiced. As adults, we elect to practice different kinds of activities. I have a rigorous workout routine. I sometimes practice yoga and meditation. I get better at some things; others I abandon.

I practiced playing the flute for ten years and became quite good. Had I not quit, I would have been first chair during my senior year in high school. My mother hoped I would continue in college. Why quit? I had been elected president of my student body and was wise enough to know I had to let at least one extracurricular activity go. You could do that back in the day. My passion for politics had exceeded my passion for music.

As I look back at what I've been deeply passionate about over the course of my life, a few things stand out—politics, exercise, working with special needs children, nature, food, and even sewing at one point. Passion can be fickle, so I ask myself, "Did you, do you, do these things with intention?"

Think about it. Professional athletes are children first. Somewhere along the line, the light bulb goes off and passion finds intention. I've often heard the story repeated. "This is what I want to do with my life. This is my passion." It's easier to measure that effort in athletics. Wins and losses, yards gained, time lost, and injury become the bars to jump. Success and failure can be quantified. If Malcolm Gladwell is correct and it requires ten thousand hours to become a master at your craft, then intentional practice is all that is required to attain your goal, whatever it is. A goal, however, may not be all there is to achieve in this life.

For years, my only goal was to be a special education teacher, all the while being my own kind of activist, political to the core. After a summer in Washington, DC, I finally bowed to my activist self. I changed my college major and set off with the intention to go to law school and become the first female Speaker of the United States House of Representatives. Five years later, when I left my job as a young and seasoned committee staffer on Capitol Hill, I began a career as a lobbyist. In a few years, after my first marriage dissolved, I seriously considered dropping out of the DC scene to enter culinary school. My father talked me out of it. I shifted into lucrative consulting opportunities and honed my skills until I was able to go out on my own. I do not regret these passions or their passing, yet I knew I was looking for a way to be and give something more. Eventually, as a mom to two young children, post 9/11, I found a home in the American Association of Naturopathic Physicians and its sister organization of medical schools that served that goal, and in tangent, Tai Sophia and Bob Duggan.

That's when I discovered practice isn't enough unless you are practicing for the sake of something much bigger than yourself. I learned intention is designed for a lifetime, not a project. I created a promise to live by and acquired the skills to maintain that promise. This crazy master's program I enrolled in was designed for me to find my figurative North Star so that I could be a healing force in the world.

Here is the promise designed at Tai Sophia: "I, Karen Howard, promise, for the sake of all beings, no matter what, wherever I am, in my present life will show as luscious opportunity to love enormously." I embedded my promise into my work on Capitol Hill. I just didn't run around vocalizing it in the halls of Congress.

The process to create this promise was rather incredible. It required engaging newly-introduced classmates in a warm and complex set of exercises to discover what others observe in their presence. Tai Sophia was a place with its own pulse. It is difficult to describe a building so full of joy (and at the same time nicknamed 'Cry Sophia'), other than to say it was authentic. It was a true reflection of its leadership—Bob, Dianne, and my dear friend Susan Duggan, Bob's second wife of thirty-two years.

I marveled at how this trio of wife, ex-wife, and husband collaborated with genuine love and respect for each other. Collectively, they had five children. Each grew up steeped in curiosity. They listened to some of our world's greatest thought leaders and were subject to constant reminders to check in with their bodies. It was Bob who pushed me out of my comfort range. Dianne, as my muse, created a space for my own creativity with music and poetry. Susan touched my soul. She always had the perfect question to ease me into awareness of my most troubled issues. Today, Susan remains one of my closest confidantes, inspiring me and loving me through this crazy-ass journey of life. Susan guides me as I make my choices and always deeply listens. In Susan's presence, life shows as a radiant, loving embrace. I'm not sure any better promise has been divined.

How do you find your promise? And once you do, how do you live your life consistently working to fulfill that promise? I can't replicate the methodology my wise teachers used. What I can do is teach you the practices I say will point you to knowing what matters enough to get you up every day and be the absolute best—the master of you.

It needs to be big. More than a dream, it's a mission.

It needs to resonate in your body, to vibrate with authority at its utterance.

It requires you to be awake and to be able to wake yourself.

It requires practice. It requires the practices in this book.

My promise has evolved over these many years. At the time it was created,

it felt solid in my body. When I would say it out loud, I literally felt planted in the ground. It felt like an epitaph I would want on my tombstone. When I shared it, people marveled. Looking back, I think that promise was only partially right. Or perhaps better said, it was right for that moment.

Now, my promise is more bold, directed, and fierce. My back straightens, my shoulders drop, and my chin squares when I speak the words, "I only do work that honors my ancestors and serves my grandchildren's grandchildren."

There is intention in this promise. It gets me up every day. When I don't listen to it, my choices are different; my body is different, there is upset, and an amazing amount of storytelling—all of which can quickly transition to physical pain. I have been given the gift of this life to make a difference. In Bob's presence, life showed up as a warm, creative vision of the future. I hope his practices, as seen through my eyes, point you to living your promise as well as he did.

Before I met Bob, I never knew anyone could be so peaceful. This was by design, not happenstance. Although he was peaceful, he was often abrupt, challenging your certitude. Imagine being asked if you were addicted to being upset. He was genuinely curious; he gently pried, not about *why* you felt a particular way, but *what* it physically felt like to be that way. He was a master at getting to the root of motivation. I watched dozens of people realize there was something (or usually someone) so important it was worth giving up a highly-tuned struggle with an in-law, mother, father, estranged friend, or neighbor.

Bob used the practices in this book as skillfully as his acupuncture needles to treat dismay and disease in his work with his patients. At the core of his teaching is the ability to be in partnership with your body, to know that you alone can find your breath at any moment and use it to flip the switch to reset before the creation of harm. The logic of the practices is irrefutably clear.

What I have learned over the years of classes and teachings is how unusual, even difficult, it is for people to be aware of how their bodies are responding to the events of life. I hear how much time they spend in their heads rationalizing, rethinking, and creating stories as though there is no body associated with this. Stress is such a major component of our lives that it's been commoditized. We accept that we need foods, supplements, and drugs to eliminate stress. Stress is a word Bob reminded us was only used as a measurement for metal until the Industrial Revolution. Ironic, isn't it?

So, I've taken the liberty to take you on this journey through the practices in an order I believe will point to the incredible value of being in a relationship with your physical self. These stories and the practices detailed will enable you to realize your own power and rewrite your story—one that brings you peace in this frenetic, often chaotic, too often cruel, and yet still magical world that we have been given the grace to live in.

In Part I, we'll focus on the wisdom of the body, placing our reliance on the brain in second place. Your body is smarter. If I don't want to be upset at what I describe as a political rant, I must first notice I'm allowing that rant to affect my breathing, my blood pressure, and the muscles in my shoulders. This means I must breathe deeply and accept the fact that each of us may choose to create a different story from the same set of facts.

I know I need to lose the hurtful words *moronic, lunatic, unbelievable,* and *I hate this* so I don't drug the people around me with their toxic effects. If I learn to keep track of all this upset I create in my body, I can identify and allay the symptoms that develop and lead to chronic pain, a trip to the medicine cabinet, or a visit to the doctor.

The practices in Part II speak to the power of language and its ability to create peace or discord. The stories we create and retell about the people we love and work with cause unnecessary suffering. Instead, I can choose to simply observe the phenomena happening before me without judgment. I also have the ability to reframe that story and give up the emotional fight that leaves me tense or drained. This practice makes it so much easier on me and those relationships. For instance, it's easier when I consider what kind of morning that 'crazy-assed driver' on the road must be having. Or when I contemplate how being raised during the Great Depression might account for what I called "the strings" my father tied to the lunch and gas money he gave me as a teenager.

I understand the difference between making a request versus a demand. The clarity I gain from understanding how the story I've created shows up in my body shines brightly when I make an effective request at work or home. Instead of sulking about my story that everything falls on my shoulders, I can use clear language to negotiate and empower everyone involved. When I do choose to make a demand, I am fully aware of the consequences.

Part III calls you to use the gifts you've been given. We all have limited time on this planet, and even the oldest of cultures teaches that we have an obligation to actively engage in positive and lasting work. Being an effective and engaged listener has added richness to my relationships and created opportunities I might otherwise have missed. This is no time to feel helpless. We have the power to design our day by choosing to be in a particular mood, and mood affects the health and well-being of everyone we come in contact with. We can practice acknowledgment, relearn how to accept each other's gifts, and feel the ease it creates in our bodies. Ask yourself, "Who is impacted by the action I take? Will it serve future generations?"

This final iteration of Bob's life's work was taught from simple worksheets. His stories and those of the thousands of people whose lives he touched have never been fully documented in prose. I've spent hours interviewing just a sampling of these people. Their stories are a central component of this book, as is mine. I've dared to take the liberty to rearrange the order of these practices. Learn them all, and it won't matter one whit. Like you and I, they are interconnected. Over time, you'll likely come to rely on one over another.

My Story

At the time of my last evening with Bob, I had put myself in a closet of sorts. Not only was I too angry to be effective in my relationship with my husband, I was also too angry to make decisions to change my life. So, I removed myself emotionally, and to the extent possible, physically. I lived in a big house, so it was a fairly easy undertaking.

During the previous summer, my mother had died rather suddenly. I got the news that she was sick while on our family vacation. She appeared to be suffering from dementia related to her illness. Being the closest geographically, I was first on the scene. My husband's response was to ask how much money was in the estate.

Unaware of the fact that a urinary infection could result in full-blown dementia, I was with her in a journey to what has to be the closest thing to hell. She transitioned to a nursing home, sharing a room with our stepfather. She died a few weeks later in late August of 2015. Ours was a troubled relationship, and I recalled her saying at my grandmother's passing that it is harder to lose one to whom you are estranged than one you love dearly. It turns out DNA is a powerful force.

Two weeks after her death, I traveled to my niece's wedding. I had my last visit with my mother-in-law, Barb, who I adored. Incapacitated by Parkinson's, a tear ran down her cheek when I told her Mom had died. As I was leaving, she miraculously spoke, telling me she would always be in my heart. I barely held my composure when I stopped at the nurses' station on my way out.

I read a poem I wrote at the wedding and waged war to be happy. I was so tightly wound that I spun out, and down, on the dance floor that night after too much to drink. Mom's funeral was next. I gave her eulogy. We lost our dog Razz in December. That night, I sobbed hard, long, and loud. When I finally went to bed, the door had been closed against the noise.

Barb died in February of 2016. I used to say I had lost the three most influential females in my life during a six-month period—my mother, my mother-in-law, and my dog Razz. Somewhere along the line, I secretly opened a private bank account to house my inheritance. As I write all of this, the tears come back, my shoulders begin to tighten, and the knot in my stomach shows itself. I have often stopped just to breathe with the memories and their effect on my body.

In that last conversation I had with Bob at his home, he looked at me with a sparkle tinged with the obvious and ringed with love.

He said, "I think it may be time to get a new story, Karen."

And so I did. Two months later, on my twenty-fifth wedding anniversary, I moved out of my home. I left my marriage, deeply committed to ensuring there would be as little upset as possible for my husband and my kids through this shift in our lives. I summoned the wisdom of my mentor and all I had learned from him. There is much more life to experience together—graduations, marriages, perhaps grandchildren, and surely more funerals. I am committed to being peaceful as we move through life.

The quality of my life depends upon the practices in this book. My physical health suffers if I go through life numb to my body. I gave myself an ulcer when I left my first husband. Every running injury I've sustained can be tied to the internal mulling over something upsetting in my life. My relationship with my children as teenagers could have escalated to the screaming confrontations of my own childhood had I not been using these practices.

I was not always successful. I'm still not, although I get better at it every day. My commitment to playing the flute for ten years resulted in me being very good at it. I've got more than sixty years of life under my belt, and I'm just now feeling like I've got this. I can successfully navigate my life with minimal upset. And when I do become upset, I can watch myself do it and bring myself back to being peaceful. Sometimes it takes seconds, and sometimes it can take days of many mini wake-ups to really let go of those feelings. Regardless, it's always better that I do this work. It's not only for me but for everyone I come in contact with including the TSA agent, the woman who won't turn right on red, or the father of my children.

PART I

**It's not that complicated.
My body is just smarter
than my mind.**

CHAPTER 1

Upset is optional, suffering is not.

There are things in life not to be ignored. Old age, sickness, death, and even birth are mandatory sufferings. Being upset is optional. You get to choose if you scream at the driver who cut you off, sob when your phone is stolen, or rant at the news on television. With practice, and lots of deep breathing, you can shed anger and frustration that serves no one, least of all you, and feel peaceful even in the midst of chaos. Here is a personal example of how this works.

It was a sunny Saturday afternoon, and I had just spent the day at an amazing, heartfelt session on the loss we experience in life and how to live the remainder well. I was headed home and on speakerphone with my daughter. Sitting at a stoplight, I am suddenly slammed from behind by another car. My first reaction was to blurt, "What the hell? There are twelve cars ahead of me stopped at a red light and this asshole just hit me!" What I saw in the rearview mirror was a man with wild, gray hair waving his hands in an agitated state.

My mouth dropped open as I observed the guy behind me who was clearly upset. I thought, "Shouldn't I be the one waving my arms around and yelling whatever he's saying?" My second thought was, "Well, it didn't seem like he hit me too hard, however, bumpers are made to absorb shock. My third thought was, "Is it safe to get out of the car for a conversation and exchange of information?"

I took one deep breath and contemplated the potential damage and the potential for road rage. It was just a quick pause that allowed me to evaluate the option of physically getting out of the car, and that's when he decided to take action and leave the scene. I made a calm choice, and I followed him with one goal. I wanted to read his license plate number to my daughter, who was still on speakerphone. I recited it to her as he ran a red light.

Have you been upset today? In the old cartoons, an angry character would hold his breath and get red in the face. Then steam would erupt from his head. Have you noticed what happens in your body when you do become upset? Sit for a moment and relive a time in the past few days when you became angry, frustrated, or totally stressed out. Put yourself back in that same place and time. Were you on the phone, at your computer, or in a room with people? Revisit the conversation, the words on the screen, or the event unfolding before you. Do you hear the conversation that drove you to become upset? What was happening to your body? Did you stop breathing? Did your body tense in a very specific place?

As the event continues in your mind, do you feel those feelings changing, moving, or intensifying? Now, see if you can let that physical response go. Release your shoulders, breathe from your belly, and relax your face and hands. If I've done my job well in asking for you to relive this moment, you've been able to recreate your physical response just by conjuring your personal thoughts.

Becoming upset is akin to cause and effect. Every time I see a toddler drop food from a high chair I'm amazed at the learning that occurs. Why wouldn't you want to do that over and over? I pick up food, I let go, and it falls to the ground. That's cool. Let's try that again. Not only that, my mom will actually pay attention when I do this and pick the stuff up. Game on!

This work is different. Contrary to popular belief, the laws of nature do not require that human actions necessitate a reaction, much less a learned or practiced reaction. We have choices we can make and the consequences of these choices have repercussions.

We can choose to rush into action spontaneously and potentially create undue hardship in our bodies. Or we can elect to proceed wisely without feeling upset and increasing our blood pressure. Several years ago, at a conference in

Anaheim, my cell phone was taken from my purse in a crowded hotel bar. The realization sent me into a tailspin. Friendly strangers were able to track my phone, which was making a steady path away from my hotel, landing several blocks away.

I elected to march off into the night by myself to find it. When I arrived at the last known site of my electronic appendage, the staff at this particular hotel let me use their computers to continue my quest. I was able to call the police. The police advised me to let them take over. They emphasized the odds of retrieval were low, even though they had concluded the phone had traveled by bike to a residence in a nearby neighborhood.

I wearily trekked back to my hotel room. Throwing in the towel, I checked out at three in the morning to get an unnecessarily early start on my flight out of LAX. I missed the police returning my phone to me by about a half hour. Rash behavior all around. This upset cost me sleep, peace of mind, and the immediate return of my phone for the long, and now exhausting, journey home.

Flash forward to the theft of my phone at yet another conference, this one in Baltimore. I was watching it from a friend's phone, exactly where I had left it, when it was turned off, never to be found. This time, I chose not to get upset. It was my fault, check. It was just a phone, check. And it was an old phone! I was off to the phone store to get a replacement with a really cute case. I also purchased an Apple Watch and wireless AirPods. It took me three and a half long hours. I shut down the store, but in my opinion, I had turned lemons into lemonade. Everything was right again in the world, and I got through the entire experience with no upset in my body.

There is no end to examples of ways we can choose to be upset or not. I knew a mother who had a flat tire on a major thoroughfare during rush hour in Washington, DC with four kids in the car. At that moment, electing to breathe deeply, she did not get upset as the cars screamed past her honking in their frustration. She understood how her upset would impact the kids. A good Samaritan stopped to help.

Amanda has declared herself "a stress eater." Working from home, she finds herself leaving her computer to forage from the kitchen cabinets on an all too regular basis. She's not happy with her work or the weight gain from "eating crap" all day long.

When asked what caused her to leave her computer, she described emails demanding short-term responses that disrupted her work and abrupt changes in deadlines. This produced stress that then resulted in a trip to the kids' section of the cabinet. For Amanda, wearing a rubber band was the solution. Each time she rose from her desk determined to forage, she snapped the band. It woke her up to the fact she let herself be triggered by an email and enabled her to stop the patterned behavior. Instead, she took that time to breathe.

No doubt, she could have chosen to purge the kitchen of all the foods she didn't really want or need to eat. Instead, a single rubber band gave her the option of letting go of the upset for the sake of something greater—her personal health and wellbeing. Not to mention a happier home for the kids when they came home from school to a mom who wasn't beating herself up for overeating their snacks for the week.

Upset is contagious. It's as contagious as the flu, with somewhat similar consequences. I was in that last half hour of my evening. The television was on low volume, and my attention was drifting slowly towards a good night's sleep. Suddenly, my cell phone rang. My daughter was upset, truly upset. The neighbor living above her had friends over, and it was loud. Really loud. Work had been extremely demanding over the past few weeks, and this day had been no exception.

Exhausted, she herself had been moving to that same ten o'clock bedtime I aspired to. Instead, we were both wide awake. I found myself listening to quite the rant about the ungrateful, spoiled tenant whose guests she could actually hear laughing as she used a broom to bang on the ceiling.

A quick assessment of her mood led me to begin by just listening to her (painful as it was) until she began to run through a list of unacceptable options for resolving the problem. As she began to spin more tightly into a tizzy, I found my own voice joining in, gaining speed and volume in response. I was physically pacing the floor, and my arms were having a conversation in tandem with my words. At one point, I yelled back at her that she might actually have to have a conversation with her neighbor. He might not even be aware how loud he and his friends were on a work night since he lived on the top floor! It was then I realized I had become infected with her upset.

I stopped moving and stopped talking. Then I realized I had stopped breathing. I took that deep breath, lowered my voice, and offered two solutions. When neither was deemed acceptable by my daughter, I put the phone on speaker. Then I went about my evening routine, brushing my teeth and turning out lights. It made me sad to know my daughter was in pain, but I was no longer allowing my body to soak it in.

In a few minutes, without my additional fuel, her fire began to dim just a little bit. We were able to say our goodnights. I texted her that she might consider writing a letter explaining her situation and slide it under her neighbor's door. She said she would, but she needed to wait for the arsenic to be included with it. I fell asleep quickly. I suspect she did not.

One last important note. Don't ever, ever, tell someone who is in the middle of being upset that it is optional. That, my daughter reminds me on a regular basis, will not work.

THE PRACTICE

Be an observer. It would be remarkable if you could go through a day, much less a week, without the opportunity to be upset. It's more likely that you are ignoring all the steps it takes to get to what you call "upset." Choosing to not be upset is best practiced by first acknowledging it happened, even if it is after the event and things have cooled down. After all, we are all beginners at this.

Set an alarm for every couple of hours to do a body check-in. Ask yourself if you feel physically tight or have an ache or pain. Think about the events prior to your check-in. Did something happen that resulted in this physical sensation? Was there a time when you stopped breathing? Document the incident with a few words on a dedicated piece of paper. My personal preference is sticky notes.

The idea is to establish an awareness that the physical sensations you feel are directly related to the events of the day. You can reverse engineer the observation. Like Amanda, define the behavior that doesn't "work" for you, whether it is mindless eating, yelling at other drivers, or maybe slamming the door on your way in or out. Determine what happened before you took that action. Don't add judgment to the story because it only compounds the upset. Consider this a fishing expedition.

Use tools to wake you up. With awareness comes power. By all means, feel free to snap yourself with a rubber band. Pick a ridiculous word, or just the word breathe, to utter in the face of seeing your upset. Share the word with your family and let them use it (again without judgment) to remind you. Learning together is an added bonus. Stopping upset in mid-sentence is a dramatic improvement over going nuclear. If you find yourself in a situation where the likelihood of upset is high, move your ring to another finger, your watch to the opposite wrist, or your phone to an unusual place. Nothing like a little awkwardness to remind you you've made a commitment to not be upset.

And remember to breathe deeply. If you suspect you are headed into a challenging situation, prepare as though you were at the starting line of a race. Ready yourself by stopping to check how you feel in your body. Set yourself by deeply breathing. Go forth with the intention to be peaceful, even in the face of upset. You don't sit at a campfire and put your hand in it, reach out to touch a hot lightbulb, or step into traffic just to see if someone will stop for you.

Your brain and body work well together when it comes to cause and effect. When you find yourself in that moment of upset, breathe, regardless of whether you are proactively creating the upset or standing in the face of it. You aren't required to react to the words and actions that set you off.

CHAPTER 2

Breathe deeply because anything worth doing is worth doing well.

.

I can't catch it.
The harder I try, the quicker it is.

We start with breath, the hottest of all stress reducers on the market at the moment. Google deep breathing, and you'll get 164 million hits. You can buy oils, tea, and jewelry. I love the breathing apps. I have one on my Apple Watch that alerts me with a warm buzz that it's time to sit back and breathe deeply for a whole sixty seconds. It's a wonderful tool to remind me deep breathing is fundamental to health. According to our guru, the Wide World Web, deep breathing is a natural painkiller that improves blood flow, increases energy levels, and improves posture. You can reduce inflammation in your body and detox at the same time while simultaneously stimulating your lymphatic system. All that, plus it improves digestion. Who am I to argue?

Take this time now as you read, to learn (or relearn) what it means to deeply breathe and the power of its ability to change your reaction. Deep breathing can literally stop you from becoming upset and stop the creation of physical pain in its tracks. It can prevent us from spewing vitriol like a virus.

Breathe before you speak, and you'll see your world is filled with stories, some of which lock you in too small of a box in which to live life fully. Breathe deeply, and you'll see the two sides to every coin and the opening for understanding. You'll understand that when you make a request of a person and offer no ability to negotiate, you are actually making a demand at which point everyone might quit breathing. You will be a better listener. You will be in a better mood too. Breathe deeply all day, and you'll be astounded how appreciative you are. You'll be able to move through your day with greater ease in your body and curiosity in your heart. Again, who am I to argue?

How many times have you been told to "just breathe"? Just do the one thing your body is quite capable of doing all on its own. In fact, it is an involuntary response. I quickly notice when I don't breathe. It's uncomfortable and becomes more so the longer I prevent myself from doing it. Frankly, I'm not a big fan of holding my breath. And, it is important to note there is more to breathing than "I am breathing" and "I am not breathing." I can be oblivious about the quality of my breathing, as I often am. It is a mistake when I allow that to happen. Being a better breather is the first and perhaps most important step to living a life without suffering. It is the first step to take when working to eliminate constant reactions to the myriad of events throughout the day. These events can consume our lives and bring feelings of resentment toward the people who have "done us wrong." This simple involuntary action, designed to sustain life, is a tool we can benefit from every moment of every day.

Let's speak to the mechanics of breathing. Wikipedia defines breathing as "the process of moving air into and out of the lungs to facilitate gas exchange with the internal environment, mostly by bringing in oxygen and flushing out carbon dioxide." When you breathe, your diaphragm pulls oxygen down through the air passages. Then, the oxygen travels through the lungs, where respiration occurs with the exchange of oxygen and carbon dioxide. The oxygen is loaded into your red blood cells, and the heart pumps that oxygen through your body. Your diaphragm comes to a moment of rest, and then the whole thing happens again.

There are different kinds of breathing. Rapid breathing can be an indicator of grave health concerns. It can be a sign of infection like pneumonia or a blood clot. It could be a warning that an anxiety or asthma attack is coming on. Shortness of breath is never a good symptom. Kudos to us, we are fairly skilled at noticing the warning signs of chronic illness associated with rapid breathing. We are far less observant of our "normal" breathing patterns and the tendency to rely on shallow breathing from our chest to support our daily functioning versus experiencing the health benefits of deep breathing from our diaphragm. Do you know the difference? Which are you doing in this very moment? Are you breathing from your chest or through your belly?

If you ever played a woodwind or brass instrument, your teacher taught you to breathe from your diaphragm. If you didn't, you would never make it through Sousa's "The Stars and Stripes Forever." If you were a swimmer, you weren't going to get far by breathing from your chest. Taking a breath with every stroke is too inefficient to be competitive.

By breathing from your belly, you are maximizing the oxygen you bring into your body and improving the efficiency of your activity. What if you were never taught how to belly breathe? The majority of us can watch our chest rise and fall with each breath. Many of us are so practiced at sucking in our bellies that the thought of releasing that muscle, the diaphragm, is counterintuitive. Let's face it, we've exchanged the corset for Spanx, for women and men. Some of us are fortunate enough to have a practice that emphasizes belly breath, like yoga or long-distance running. Ask yourself what happens once you leave your yoga mat or take off your running shoes. Do you go back to breathing from your chest?

THE PRACTICE

Wake up to your belly breath! Place one hand on your chest and the other on your belly. Sit and breathe naturally. Observe. Is your chest rising? Or is it your belly you feel moving? Are you talking to yourself about that belly fat? Give yourself a hall pass, and let that go in this moment. This work is too important for vanity to get in the way.

Start again. This time, place both your hands on your belly. Breathe deeply and slowly into that diaphragm as you feel your hands rise. It's good to exaggerate your belly inhale for learning purposes, though it need not feel forced. Now exhale for as long as you can without forcing it. Practice this. In your head, use a slow count to three or four at your own pace for both your inhale and exhale. It may take some time to become connected to the rise and fall of your belly with your breath.

Congratulations on this effort. You now know exactly what it feels like to be "in your body." You've silenced that running dialogue in your head. Sometimes thoughts can feel like the ending of a pharmaceutical ad, a running list of warnings about all the terrible things that could happen today. It is so easy to get caught up in that swirl, spinning on the head of a pin, almost frenetic in an attempt to keep everything moving forward smoothly. When something does go haywire (and it will), it can be dizzying.

Imagine that moment when you've had just about enough. When the kids are yelling in the back seat of the car or the person in your meeting is telling you again why something just won't work. When you walk in the house after a long day, there are shoes and coats all over the entry hall and the kitchen dishes are still in the sink. The television is blaring in the family room, and no one is watching it. The dog, or maybe it was the cat, has thrown up on the floor.

Now, visualize a stop in time. A split second of complete silence that allows you to take a deep breath from the belly and slowly exhale. Do it again. Do it a third time. What the hell, give it one more go. Four deep breaths, in and out, belly moving. How is your body now? Do you feel more at ease and able to move forward without the tightness in your jaw, the clenching of your fists, or the pulling of your hair? Ask yourself who benefits if you don't let loose in a tumbleweed of fury? Everyone.

Here is a real-world example of the impact of this practice in action. We'll call them Jenna and Parker to protect their privacy.

I'm in the pediatrician's office with Parker, who's not feeling well.

The doctor said, "He's late on his vaccine. So while you're here, we should give him his flu shot."

And I said, "Well, you know, he's sick. So we're not going to do the flu shot today."

She didn't let it go and proceeded to bring it up at least one to two more times. So, I lost it. I got upset. Raising my voice, I told her to back up. I was thinking, "No way are you gonna pump chemicals into my son when he's sick."

That's when Parker calmly interrupted and said, "Everyone stop. Everybody breathe. Mama, calm down."

I just looked at him and thought, "You're right."

He does this often. I can stub my toe or just be in a passionate conversation with his dad about the house, and he's like, "Whoa, whoa, whoa, come on, breathe. You breathe, you breathe."

He uses this practice on himself, too. He was recently in the bath, and he said, "I'm trying to breathe, trying to breathe. I made a lie, Mama. Sorry, I made a lie."

I asked, "Parker, what's the deal with making a lie?"

"I don't know," he said. "But my heart beats fast. Can you help me stop my heart from beating fast? Then I won't make a lie."

At four years old, he sat in the bathtub with the realization that he can shift a feeling in his body by telling himself to breathe so his heart will slow down.

We have taught him this skill. He's afraid of bees.

When we come across any I say, "Parker, don't panic. Just breathe."

One day, I gave him a quick pinch and told him that's what it would feel like when the bee stings. "It's okay to be afraid, but you don't need to panic," I said, "and you won't if you breathe."

So, yes, we taught him that the words coming out of his mouth and the thoughts in his head have an impact on his body. That he can change that by breathing. It's definitely made a difference. And now Parker is my teacher.

This is our first practice. If you take nothing else away from this book, let it be the practice of deeply breathing. Malcolm Gladwell says you need to practice ten thousand hours to become a master at a specific task. Here's the good news—by the age of sixty, I will have spent 525,600 hours breathing.

Clearly, I know how to breathe. Now, I just need to achieve Master Breather status by using my diaphragm. You won't yell in upset if you are belly breathing. I believe it is physically impossible to do so. Imagine a life of not yelling or being yelled at.

Belly breathing creates a physical release. Shoulders go down, eyes soften, headaches ease, and the body returns to equilibrium. It is a peaceful feeling. Belly breathing is essential for every practice in this book. We hold our tension and stress throughout our body, causing all kinds of pain and discomfort. This is suffering we can often eliminate by breathing.

Design reminders to use on a daily basis. Use your breathing app if you have one. Set the schedule to intersperse your day with breathing breaks at the beginning, middle, and end. No app? Sticky notes are always handy. Place one on your bathroom mirror. Make sure you have one in your car. Place it in the center of the steering wheel, perhaps where the horn is. They should just read "breathe." If you end up ripping it off when hitting the horn, then that should wake you up in the moment.

Screen savers are a great way to highlight any practice. Start with the word breathe. Each time you see it, take that deep belly breath. Meetings are the perfect place to practice this skill. Unlike constantly checking your phone, no one will actually know you are using time for yourself during a meeting. If you doodle, use the word breathe as your centerpiece. If you find yourself in a less-than- productive or even slightly upsetting conversation, sit back in your chair with your feet planted on the ground. Relax your shoulders and start that belly breath.

You'll never regret this pause in time and space, but you could easily regret your own words if you don't. If you are running the meeting, cooking dinner, rushing through the store, or running late to pick up the kids, you are going to think you can't make time for this. Remember, you are already breathing. You just need to breathe a bit deeper to effectively silence that distracting voice of worry or anticipation. The stress that we eat keeps us from sleeping and stirs the acids in our stomachs.

We all know what happens when you quit breathing completely. Don't think there isn't a price to pay for not effectively using your breath, or for that matter, practicing any of the tools in this book. Can you choose to walk through the day peacefully and at ease? Or will you stew like the proverbial pot ready to boil over until it does? This is your first step to having a healthy relationship in your body. Notice I say *in* your body versus *with* your body. Obviously, you can't be without your body.

CHAPTER 3

Words are like drugs. Some are healing; others inflict pain.

Word Wall:

I can't stand her…. what a lame excusE… I hate you…
This—is—impossible… With all due respect… *that is the
worst decision…* I'm so weak… WHAT a moron!

Anyone who has ever heard a child speak their first word
truly understands the power of speech. The utter joy of
two syllables flooding through your body, eyes brightening,
heart pumping, arms outreached, perhaps with a tear in your
eye. Your physical response to the syllables etch the memory
of the first "Mama" or "Dada" in your brain.

Saying "I love you" and meaning it, or the proposal of
marriage, are memories that revive physical feelings. They
bring your body back to that moment. You may feel your

chest expand and your face relax. You may even create one of those "single tears" as you relive the moment.

The same is true for words that inflict pain because words are drugs. They can harm or heal, and over time, become a part of the story of who you are, warranted or not. Words create a somatic response in your body, electrifying your nervous system and causing a physical response to the sounds.

My mother had a very large personality. While the world was her domain, she used the kitchen as her personal salon, holding court with her friends on the phone and creating the parties and meals she was famous for. It was also her emotional gymnasium. When something was wrong, you knew it. Kitchen cabinet doors were slamming shut and pots were rattling the rafters. To this day, the slamming of a kitchen cabinet is far more than startling to me. I have a physical reaction that tightens my entire body and leaves me standing upright and at attention, waiting for the next thing to happen, just as I did as a child. We are so very practiced at communicating that we can do so even without speech, all of it impacting our bodies.

Social media embraces this learned behavior in our bodies. We can ruin someone's day, start a campaign, or even change the course of history by screaming 280 capitalized characters. The power of being heard has never been so obvious, and yet we can be so careless in its sharing. The old adage, "Think before you speak," hasn't lost its relevance. We just aren't using it. We see it in our children and the use of bullying, electronic and otherwise. The damage can last a lifetime.

Don't think that the impact of words dissipates with age. My friend at boot camp tells me I look strong and thin, and the space in my chest feels more open. A week earlier, my brother's mere insinuation that I could lose some weight caused my brow to furrow and my shoulders to tense. That friend in your office who never dances when you go out? Tell a child whose nickname is "Moose" she is clumsy just enough times, and she'll believe it, becoming a grownup who avoids any activity only a graceful child could have undertaken. Words. They can limit our joy, keep us awake at night, and flood our bodies with chemicals and neurotransmitters. Words can, and do, damage your health.

Revisit the last time you were upset. Did your body tense? Maybe your face turned red or your brow furrowed? Perhaps you clenched your hands or waved them energetically in the air—or both. It's distinctly possible you raised your voice in anger and shared a series of loud, unpleasant, or even hateful sounds in the form of words.

If words are indeed drugs, you just sneezed in the face of your colleague, wife, husband, or child. Maybe you are one of those people who can let loose a barrage of words without any upset and feel perfectly calm afterward, oblivious to the physical despair left in your wake. More likely, however, you also feel the effects—perhaps fatigue, an ache in your chest, or a pain in your neck or back. With a simple utterance, you can become Linus, dragging the contagion of your words and actions through the hallways for others to breathe in. Disturbing the peace is a criminal offense caused by excessively loud noise. Take notice of the impact you are having on the health status of others.

My Story and Argument with Caleb

I was so grateful when Caleb called me to let me know I was late for my own meeting that morning. Time had gotten away from me, and I let myself emerge into an issue unrelated to our business at that moment. When I got on the call, I quickly apologized for being late. That's when he unleashed at me. He chastised me in front of our colleagues, demanding an update on the product under development.

I had heard this vicious tone before, though never directed at me. I sat back in my chair with a realization that his words had an intention, but I was too distracted by the vitriol to ascertain what was expected from me. I took several deep breaths. When I spoke, I used a measured and flat tone, as if to counter the chaos I sensed growing on the other end of the line.

"You know," I replied calmly, "exactly where we are in the process because you were on last week's call."

There appeared to be nothing that could stop him. "Hey, Karen," he continued, "we don't need your negativity."

He spoke with acerbic intensity as I explained that some of the design elements we had received were less than satisfactory.

I was thinking that I'm the least negative person I know! Despite a calm demeanor, I felt relief come when he left the call.

"That was not okay," my remaining colleague commented.

"No, it was not," I replied.

I began to wonder if this was a project I wanted to continue.

I had watched Caleb's words impact my body chemistry. The tingling in my head seemed to alert my body into an upright position. Sitting back in my chair, I remembered to breathe, avoiding upset in the moment. I chose my words carefully. This is not about being nice or being politically correct. It is a call to develop habits of clear and effective speech so that your words aren't causing physical harm.

Months earlier, shortly after the launch of this project, I had shared the following thoughts and concerns with Caleb about how things were going. His patience was wearing thin.

"I know you are very aware you can't do the work of this project all by yourself. I also suspect if you had your choice, you would prefer to do this project all by yourself."

He concurred.

"Let's work together to make sure your time is spent on the things you excel at and that you can be comfortable delegating responsibilities to the team you have assembled."

I could have said, "You are micromanaging this project to death by insisting you be a part of every conversation and decision. We'll never get this business open unless you change."

My choice of words was designed to engage him in conversation, not to blame or change him. In my experience, effective words lead to effective actions.

Caleb had chosen words that silenced a group of people on the phone. He misused the limited time that our very busy and invested team had to offer that project. His words hurt the project. His words hurt me. So, I did what most good friends and business partners would do, I retreated. Funny, I don't like being hurt, especially when I don't feel like I did anything to warrant being yelled at. I pulled back and away in an effort to stay safe. Not a particularly effective way to lead us to success, but at the moment, I determined the careful selection of minimal language was the optimal choice. I had been sneezed on.

I made several choices during that call and in the days afterward. The first was to be an observer in that moment and not engage in a discourse of discomfort. I chose not to fight back with my own words. Instead, I elected to observe the context and assess in real-time the potential for collateral damage in the working relationships of the people on the phone that day I wanted to power through and maintain a sense of calm and stability for the sake of the people engaged in this work. I chose to not get upset. Until I didn't.

I realized I was carrying a story about what had happened throughout the day. I concluded that ignoring my upset was the same thing as being upset. I struggled for two solid days to let go of the physical effect those words had in my body. The tightness in my shoulders and chest was intense, as though I was preparing for a boxing match. The shallowness of breath came back when I walked through the conversation in my head, pacing as I considered my options. In the end, I chose silence while I worked to find words for having a peaceful conversation about a very difficult subject. Six days later, I found my response.

"Last Wednesday can't happen again, Caleb. When you attack me, you hurt me. You also risk the confidence of a group of people who believe in you and this project. We chose to lead this together because we love and trust each other, and I would rather sacrifice the project than our friendship."

Be mindful of what you speak. If uncertain, choose silence until you have clear, simple, and effective words.

I will add that six days was too long to let all that swim around in my body, alternating between resolute in my opposition and desolate in disposition. If there is a next time, as there is likely to be, I promise myself to take effective action with words and regain peace in my body much faster. Equally important, I will remember my words are indeed drugs to be delivered for healing. Human beings do not harm.

At a time in society when we are being bombarded by vitriol, this is work that empowers and feeds the soul. Choosing your words, that old practice in dire need of dusting off, will open doors and silence the slamming of kitchen cabinets. This is about learning the art of using words to open possibility instead of fostering complaint or gossip. It's about being curious and asking questions instead of snapping to judgment. It's about acknowledging the power of language to heal or harm in business, at home, and throughout your life. It's about living a peaceful life.

If you have any doubt in the physical power of words, consider the last time you apologized to someone. The odds are in your favor that it was the use of certain words you chose that had an unfavorable impact warranting an apology. Now think about the last time someone said something to you that caused upset. How did you respond physically? Did you "sneeze" words back at the person with a red face, tightness in your chest, and ringing in your ears? Did you physically leave the room? Did you find water leaking from your eyes? We aren't that different from children on the playground. One child calls another stupid, and the immediate reaction is tears. Words are drugs to our bodies.

THE PRACTICE

Catchphrases and shorthand messages can imperil relationships or, at the least, stop a conversation dead in its tracks. These words lack curiosity. "We need to talk" is surely the equivalent of "We have a problem." I know that because my throat tightens and my breathing gets very, very shallow. "Can I see you for a minute?" invites a buzzing sensation on the top of my head.

And those are just a few of our universal verbal alarms. Each of us with our own unique background brings a history of practice, our own kitchen cabinet door slamming, as to how words affect us. Think about the last time someone, a parent perhaps, used your full name at the start of a sentence. Think about when you called your child by his or her full name. There was an intention in that language. We also have a language of love, perhaps less practiced, that is an equally, if not a more, powerful drug. So how do we become awake to the words we use, design communication with intention, and inspire great conversation?

Some of the most effective communicators I know work with preschoolers, for which I am eternally grateful. In my sister-in-law's care, little ones are steeped in the learning of language and how to tend to one another's feelings. They learn some words are not to be used because they hurt feelings. She demonstrates that everyone is afforded an opportunity to be heard. Kindness is key, and certain actions, like the throwing of toys, are not allowed. We start today with a refresher course for everyone over five years of age.

Be a good listener. Listen to the words spoken to you during the day that trigger a physical reaction in you—both good and bad. Some may be delivered habitually. Others may be shared out of frustration, anger, or even fear. When a word hits your body with a force that causes physical discomfort, ask yourself questions about your response. It's possible that no harm was intended. Your boss/husband/best friend might have been reacting to something that happened earlier in the day that had no relationship with you. It's also possible this person hit one of your historical triggers and slammed a cabinet door. Just be curious and open to the possibility that there is more than one way to hear those words. Take notes (meaning write them down) and pair them with your physical responses.

Take time to observe other people's conversations in meetings at the office, on the subway, with the TSA agent, and in line at the grocery store. You may notice a physical change in the two people talking. The change could be voices rising as a conversation becomes adversarial or direct eye contact and smiles when there is an expression of gratitude between two people.

When you hear "thank you" from one person to another, does it resonate somewhere in your body? When you listen to someone chastise the clerk at the checkout counter, where in your body does it land? Are you creasing your brow and tightening certain muscles if you become irritated? If so, this is evidence that the words used are drugging not only the partners engaged in conversation but the observers as well. Write these words down along with your physical responses.

Listen to yourself. Now begin taking note of your own use of language. Create a word bank, an accounting of the words that you use the most, for good and bad. You can literally build your own word wall. The more you use a word, the larger it becomes. Start with two words. The first should be one you know your body feels good about. Mine is the word "grateful." Then pick another that you might want to use less. Mine would be "moron." My rationale for using it is that I often refer to myself as a moron; so, what the heck? No harm done. And then I remind myself, "No go, girlfriend." Go through the day and see how you manage those two words. Continue to build your word wall.

After you've built your word wall. We have a list of words we train our children not to use, beginning at a very early age. They are generally words considered verboten for the young and, sadly, acceptable in adult conversation. Think about that concept as you compare your two lists and your growing word wall. Revise the verboten accordingly.

We don't like our children to call each other stupid. We frown at language that demeans others, and at the same time, we can quickly resort to name-calling in a heated conversation. We can be dismissive, saying, "There's no time for that today, Roger." We often rush through conversations for the sake of productivity at the expense of collaboration and receiving valuable input from others.

We gossip and use hurtful language around appearance, clothing, weight, and intelligence. This language can land so solidly in the physical body of the person we are denigrating that it can create physical discomfort for him or her. It could result in long-term relational damage, and it could possibly land you in the human resource office. We believe if it's not heard, it doesn't hurt. Perhaps that is true. That said, if you are committed to being an effective communicator, this is a perfect place to start your new language. It is virtually impossible not to speak or communicate, whether in writing or verbally, in your waking hours. So, if you are going to drug people all day long, choose between curiosity vs. inquisition, silence vs. anger, and kindness vs. gossip.

Be artful in your word choice. There is an art to conversation that could use some refreshing, beginning with the understanding that every word has an impact. Over time, I've actually ceased to use certain words altogether, including the word "but," which serves to limit conversation and/or negate the point originally made. "I like her, but…" generally signals an unkindness is next. "It's a good idea, but…" will likely end with a statement of limitation rather than possibility. I no longer use "try," electing to channel my inner Yoda, reminding myself it can be done or it can't. There simply is no try. The same with "should."

"Don't be a weeny," I tell myself. "Make a choice."

I've added the use of specific words. When relevant, I close many of my emails with the salutation, "With gratitude." I ask many questions when I'm truly uncertain whether I understand the speaker. When someone says, "I simply don't have the time to address your concern," I could conclude that it is meant to denigrate the importance of my request. Instead, I elect to make no judgment and use words that leave the door open for conversation. "I understand. Perhaps there is a time later today or tomorrow when you and I can discuss this?" This gets me closer to my answer than sulking off with my head down and a sinking feeling in my stomach.

Curiosity has led to many interesting conversations with people I know and strangers in lines and on planes. Sometimes, I purposely share that I practice being a "healing presence in the world through my words and actions." No one knows what the hell I mean. Just the use of those words strung together generates some interesting dialogue.

Acknowledge and adjust. When I make a mistake along the way (as we all do), I've learned issuing an apology gets me back on track. Now that I understand how words can generate enormous upset for me and my partners in life and work, I can accept being unsuccessful now and then—as long as I remember to take a quick pause to consider how my body is responding to my slipup.

- I first acknowledge I've used words that harm.

- I then take note of the physical feelings I am experiencing. For me, it's usually a sinking feeling in my stomach, and I have probably quit breathing.
- After several deep breaths, I can elect to issue my apology, perhaps reframing the conversation as well.

I remember the countless times I "shared" my disappointment with my kids when they were younger. The loud delivery of words steeped in judgment accomplished little. I learned that silence accompanied by deep breathing was a much more effective tool than losing my temper and spewing vitriol. It enabled my ability to listen and actually choose the words I wanted with care. I take comfort in the fact that these physical responses in my body—ones I've come to know so well—serve as my teachers. They are my guidepost, my reminders, to return to being peaceful in my body, breathing, and eliminating any upset. This allows me to be that healing presence for the family, friends, colleagues, and strangers I interact with daily.

CHAPTER 4

Five symptoms that point to illness and pain.

"Thirty years ago, Charlie said to me, 'I never thought asthma would be my friend. Now I use it to remind me to pay attention to my food, sleep, exercise, and emotions.'"
—Bob Duggan

We live in a mechanistic world where the head and body are seemingly separate. Medications are prescribed to treat conditions that are now commonly labeled diseases in medical parlance. Osteoarthritis will affect virtually all of us as we age—it is a condition of aging. Yet, the pharmaceutical industry has labeled this condition as a disease to be treated with pharmaceutical medications. Restless legs syndrome (RLS) is a "condition that causes an uncontrollable urge to move your legs, usually because of an uncomfortable sensation." It is not a disease. Asthma is defined as "a respiratory condition marked by spasms in the bronchi of the lungs, causing difficulty in breathing. It usually results from an allergic reaction or other forms of hypersensitivity." It, in itself, is not the disease it has been labeled.

Our modern-day philosophy is to medicate our symptoms. We seek to eliminate the pain from arthritis, reduce the twitching from RLS, and open up air passages to allow easier breathing for asthma. Conventional medicine does not interest itself in identifying what is causing painful inflammation, figuring out the underlying reasons causing a leg to twitch, or studying the events leading to an asthma attack. Treatments are rarely prescribed for the entirety of even one body system, much less a whole human being who eats, sleeps, exercises, and emotes in a way uniquely their own. It is as though we have no control, no ability to find our way to health without drugs.

Bob shared a story of how he showed his client, we'll call him Charlie, a way to live with asthma, not as a disease, but as a way to manage the quality of the life he was living. Noticing his symptoms as they appeared along the path to an asthma attack enabled Charlie to take more control of his condition.

We all have symptoms that fail to meet the threshold of requiring a doctor's appointment, such as digestive issues, sharp or dull muscle aches and pains, lack of sex drive, or sleepless nights. Most of these symptoms are ignored and left unattended. Bob taught us that experiencing a notable series of symptoms can be directly linked to a chronic health condition. A lack of sleep might show up as a specific pain in your knee, back, or neck. Left unattended, that specific pain could result in an additional four or five symptoms, let's say, a headache over the eyes. The headache could then become the focus of your day, and without being aware, you could be restricting your fluid intake. If you restrict your fluid intake, you may now be facing a full-blown migraine headache.

Hypothetical? Perhaps. And yet, Bob helped his client Charlie discover when he neglected eating the right food, getting enough sleep and exercise, and monitoring his emotions, he would experience an asthma attack. By monitoring and checking in on a regular basis, he could actually thwart an attack. He could control the onset of the symptoms—turn things on and off.

The challenge here is for you to define the four or five minor symptoms that come and go in your body. These should be symptoms that get better or worse, not permanent ones like the loss of hearing or an actual medical diagnosis like cancer.

It's time to get to know your body for the sake of its health. You can shake the need for over-the-counter sleep aids, improve your quality of life, and reduce the long-term impact of debilitating conditions. Reduce the number of migraines, asthma attacks, and sleepless nights by getting to their root cause. While the process may not completely eliminate your personal health issue, it is highly likely that you'll be much better versed in what you need to stop the escalation of your body's response and reduce your need for doctor's visits.

When Bob taught this practice, I was asked to write down my symptoms in the order they appeared. It was a request that baffled me, so it began a three-month journey to define my five symptoms. At first, I drew a blank. Nada. I could not define one symptom I experienced that did not require me to seek medical help, much less five that occurred in a specific order. There was nothing that would result in a lack of sleep or appetite, pain or discomfort. I pride myself in how I take care of my body, and I seldom rely on the conventional medical system for care.

"The only thing I consistently do for myself," I proudly reported, "is my monthly visit to the chiropractor." When pushed as to why I went to the chiropractor, I replied, "I have a leg that is slightly shorter than the other, and I have flat feet."

I was advised that, because I was a runner, it resulted in hip pain. Therefore, I got regular adjustments so I could continue to live my healthy lifestyle.

Bob asked one particular question that showed me a path toward defining my symptoms. "Is there a consistent response in your body to upset?"

After a bit of thought, I replied, "Yes. I get a knot in my stomach, just below the breastbone."

And that's how my exploration into my five symptoms began.

It's a tight knot, ready at any moment to remind me I'm headed into upset. In the quest to identify my five symptoms, I let myself get to know them over the next few weeks. I said "hello" to it when I would finish a particularly difficult work conversation. I could feel it sitting all tucked up in my abdomen, practically throbbing in its element. After a while, I realized it was almost like another appendage, and I started to refer to it as my friend. I discovered that when I practiced breathing, I could make it go away. It was then that I began to understand the true power of my body and its abilities. It was also around that time that symptom two became obvious—this knot just to the left of my right shoulder blade. That's when I got really curious.

There were days, usually close to my monthly chiropractic appointment, when I would wake up with numbness in my right hand. I had associated it with the whole uneven nature of my body. I knew that it would be relieved with the skilled treatment I received, which included a wrist adjustment. What if these symptoms were related?

And then it happened. One morning, I sat at my desk observing my stomach knot playing tennis with the spot in my back. In an instant, I felt a sharp pain shoot up and land at the base of my skull on the right side. I immediately stopped any effort to resolve these issues. Be damned, deep breathing! Instead, I embarked on a personal study to see what would happen next. Sure enough, that neck pain quickly transmitted through my arm, numbing my hand during my sleep. Not long after that, the pain in my hip was back, and I was fully inflamed for my monthly visit to the chiropractor.

Karen's Symptoms:

1. A knot in my upper abdomen that left unattended results in a...
2. Knot under the right shoulder blade. My persistence in ignoring said knot causes a...
3. Pain in the neck just below my skull on that pesky right side.
4. During the night, the pain radiates down my arm and into my hand.
5. I awake and go for a run with a pain in the hip, which I suspect results from muscle tension and nerve response.

It took three months for me to figure out this scenario and begin the process of reverse engineering my body's responses. What I've learned is that if I notice the knot in my stomach, I can breathe it away, literally. If I do not tend to it fairly quickly, the knot in my shoulder blade appears, and it is virtually impossible to not notice.

That said, there have been times when I'm so engrossed in a project that I do "wake up" to find myself suffering from a neck pain. However, it is highly unusual for me to allow the progression past that point. In fact, I am so highly attuned to my symptoms that I can actually summon my "friend," a.k.a. my teacher, at will. Deep breathing can, and does, effectively stop this process at any point.

I still go to my chiropractor on a regular basis, but for different reasons. I go because I believe in self-care, just as I choose to eat a healthy diet, take breaks when sitting for extended times at my desk, and exercise regularly. I also get a kick-ass massage once a month and see my acupuncturist for regular tune-ups.

There are times when I am experiencing pain or discomfort at these treatments. An extensive travel schedule, coupled with a heavy workload, topped off with a lack of awareness and failure to breathe deeply, are the factors I associate with these pains. At a recent chiropractic visit, when I was in particular discomfort, I had to smile when my doctor commented that it's not like I do this to myself. I actually had done this to myself.

THE PRACTICE

Conduct an inventory. The path to finding your symptoms and putting them in the order they disappear is its own journey. Begin with noting the changes that come and go in your body over seven days. Jot down these seemingly random sensations and feelings. Remember, these are symptoms, not diagnoses or permanent healthcare issues like losing your hearing or receiving injuries from an accident. These are ticks and twitches that consistently come and go.

It's the sensation that causes you to reach for ibuprofen or the stomach issue that keeps you from going out. It could be a throb in your head or knee. Even the ache you associate with a forecast of rain may play a role.

Be your best at observing. Explore the subtleties of each of these sensations. See how they change, ebb, or intensify. Are some seemingly random, while others are familiar? Catalog what you are learning, creating columns for rarely, often, or surprising.

Construct your hypothesis. Before you act to eradicate the issue by treating it, question your understanding of the onset. What might have happened before this headache? How was your sleep? Could the headache be from something you ate or drank, or might it be muscle-related? Perhaps you aren't drinking enough water. Maybe it is all of these things combined. Consider whether there is consistency in how the symptoms come and go. Perhaps you see the ebb and flow while you are observing the events themselves. Place your findings in the inventory.

Test your theories. Pick a symptom and see if you can make it go away. Use breath, rest, sustenance, or perhaps meditation. Are you in charge of it? How do you make it come and go? Are you breathing deeply, or have you returned to a shallow breath from your chest?

Don't give up. The rewards are significant and potentially have the power to reduce your personal pain and improve your health status. Chronic fatigue, skin conditions, mild depression, headaches, and backaches cause us to reach for the bottles with the childproof caps. If you are curious and thoughtful, it is possible to find linkages—symptoms that line up like stepping stones to a full-blown event, attack, or chronic condition.

PART II

**If Shakespeare said,
"All the world's a stage,"
how can we use language
to live the best life possible?**

CHAPTER 5

There is story and there is phenomena. Know the difference and save a relationship.

"There's only what happened. All the rest you get to make up." Bob Duggan.

H umans are phenomenal storytellers. Even in the days when survival was paramount, the cavemen and women made time to document their hunts on walls. Indigenous populations shared their entire history and culture from generation to generation through oral history— an art form rarely practiced in modern culture with its reliance on technology.

Friends and families gather for weddings and funerals, graduations and birthdays, holidays and reunions, sharing family history and creating new lore through the telling of stories. Story can be a beautiful thing. Story can also cause enormous suffering. A story is what you say about something that happened. The phenomena is the "happening" or the event. The story is what the teller wants it to be. It's an interpretation, someone's point of view, and that is where things can go haywire.

We walk in story much of our day.

A crazy guy just hit me from behind while I was stopped at a red light!

Phenomena: I got hit from behind by a man in a car. Now he's waving his hands around his head.

Story: He's crazy.

Sara just walked by me and didn't say hi! She must be mad at me for not returning her email from yesterday.

Phenomena: Sara walked by me without saying a word.

Story: She's mad at me.

There is no need to judge ourselves harshly for our ability to create a story. We humans are highly practiced at deduction. And, frankly, "judgment" is often a story about the phenomena experienced. The question is, "Can you notice when you are creating a story and the effect your story has on others and yourself?"

Here is an example of story versus phenomena that Bob shared with all his students. Bob's mother died when he was three. She went to the hospital to give birth and never came home. Those are the simple facts, the phenomena. Bob could have grown up with many versions of a story about her death. He could have lived with the story of her tragic death and his loss.

Instead, his father told him while most boys have their mothers with them, he was a very privileged young man to have his mother sitting at the right hand of God, watching out for him.

"You're protected," he added. "You're a special kid for the rest of your life."

That was the story Bob lived with his entire life. The stories we choose to tell in this life have enormous consequences.

As Bob would say, "You will create story. The question is, is it a story big enough to live in?"

When I was in fifth grade, my mother and father sat me down to tell me that Dad was not my real father. I was three when they married, and I had a biological father who lived in St. Louis. Now, I was told, Dad wanted to adopt me and become my legal parent. What I had lived with as a phenomenon was in fact all story. And, it was a story that my parents made so big for me that I experienced absolutely no upset with the revelation. Dad was simply, and wonderfully, my Dad. I was not afraid during the legal proceedings, even when I was questioned in what I remember to be enormous, dark, and solemn chambers by a very formidable judge. I went back to school that day and simply announced to my classmates that I had been adopted. Conversation over.

Is there a misunderstanding in your life that has damaged a relationship at home or work? With friends or family? The goal of this practice is to observe the difference between the story about a "misunderstanding" and the "damage" it causes versus the phenomena—the actual events, words, and actions that occur.

My mother used to tell the story of me as a baby touching a hot burner on the stove. I've never touched a hot burner again. The power of understanding phenomena is apparently something even a baby gets. The implications of creating and living in a story are equally powerful and potentially as dangerous as touching a hot stove.

Think back to my friend Caleb on that phone call spewing a virus over hundreds of miles. Remember how I maintained my calm at the moment, only to later fret, upset for days in the aftermath? I got out of that upset by realizing I had a choice. I could rationalize his behavior by telling myself stories.

Perhaps, I thought, *he is upset because of the enormous pressure to get this project off the ground. Or maybe things at home are not going well.*

That could very well be true, I told myself, *but I can't assume that.*

I next moved to a story that managing multiple jobs, as both of us did, can result in too much stress. I immediately realized that was likely to be true, and that's mostly my story. I then considered his lack of organizational skills that could result in his feeling out of control. I added the fact that he would rather be doing the work without anyone's help and resented the fact he needed me.

Wow, I thought. *That's either incredibly insightful or totally bodacious of me. I really am quite the storyteller.* In the end, I pushed all that aside and stuck with the facts and the phenomena. Then, I was able to move forward with him.

THE PRACTICE

So, here's the question: How do I make myself aware that I'm in a story? What is the practice?

Nail down the facts. Pick a recent scenario when you were upset. Tease out the actual details about what happened in those moments. Write down the actual phenomena, just the facts.

Identify your upset. As you relive the events, identify the moment when you found yourself upset and the physical response you created in your body. What was the conclusion you came to that led to you being upset? Determine whether it was the story or the phenomena that produced the upset.

Compare and contrast. As you consider the story you created using the facts you identified, see if you can create four more versions of the story. Ask yourself what happens to the upset in your body as you switch to a different version of the story.

Sara walked by me in the hallway this morning without speaking. My stomach tightened.
I think she is mad at me, or...
- *Maybe she's distracted and just didn't see me.*
- *It's been a hellacious week, so I'll give her the space she might need.*
- *Maybe she's just running late for her next meeting.*
- *I'll check in with her later today to make sure everything is okay.*

Make a point of finding one story a day, just for the sake of identifying it. It's really quite easy since, as humans, we do this all day long. Again, there is no judgment. Frankly, our lives are one big story, some of which we will carry with us for life.

My daughter went off to her first day of preschool. She cried, hung onto her dad for dear life, and essentially begged to go home. At least, that's the story I heard since I was out of town on business, and it's certainly the story she continues to tell. I had a choice on what to do with that information. At the time, I created my own story about being The Missing Parent and The Bad Mommy. I've let that story go, but I'm not sure my daughter has. However, she is a highly adjusted and successful young woman now. Other stories carry more risk and have the potential for a lasting impact on generations.

Crystal's Story

My maternal grandmother died in December. She lived in Ohio, where I was raised. I'm a black woman from a family of the whitest white people ever. They are Christian Republicans from Midwestern Ohio. Obviously, I'm not quite like them. I was adopted when I was six weeks old. So I had lots of stories and feelings about going back to Ohio. I knew I would go because it was my grandmother, and I loved her. She was always really good to me. Despite our differences, I know she loved me.

So, I got in the car to go back to Ohio. I was driving on the turnpike, listening to some podcast (Tony Robbins, I think), and I saw the big Ohio sign. I immediately felt this need to be a different person. I created an image of being covered in armor to protect me because I was going into the place where hurtful things happened.

It was raining, as it seems to always be in Ohio, and I felt the stories beginning anew in my body. I remember talking with my Uncle Butch, a Trump supporter and a Fox News fan. He never treated me differently and used to take me out in his tractor.

"How," I wondered, "will I be with Uncle Butch when he's clearly made decisions I can't understand?"

When I arrived, I asked myself, "Who am I in this room? I don't think any black people are members of this church."

And then I looked at all the pictures on picture boards that included my family, and I realized that these are my people. I can't go around being mad at Trump supporters or people with the Confederate flag because these are my people. I don't know why they love the Confederate flag. I just assumed you have that flag because you don't like people who look like me. How the hell do I know what you like? I never asked you. I just saw the flag and said, "Bye-bye, buddy!"

I had to let the armor down. These are my people, by choice or not. I can't walk around infecting them with these little arrows of blame I shoot, only to be surprised when they react in a way I predicted.

Two weeks ago, I was with them again, this time in Kentucky, for my nephew's wedding. It was raining, but I didn't need the armor to cross the state line this time. My daughter was the flower girl at this wedding, so I made up another story.

"Isn't this nice," I thought, "a cute, little random black girl is the flower girl? How inclusive of them."

I've got a little chip on my shoulder, failing to realize that this is my nephew, who I've known since before he was born. I love this guy. He's stood up for me in public. He's the blond-haired, hipster beard guy. He's my guy. And there I was, mother of the flower girl and aunt to the groom, except people kept asking me who I was. I grew indignant, yet another story instantaneously pushing me into suffering when, in fact, I didn't have a neon light flashing over my head with my name. So, how could they know who I am?

The same thing happens when I'm in Whole Foods and a "Just In Front" (that's a person who is oblivious to my presence) stands between me and the shelf. I create a story about the white lady who doesn't see me. Maybe she did, and maybe she didn't. Maybe she needs to pee, and she's just in a hurry. I have no way of knowing.

I've become a story ninja. I catch myself more quickly now. I now catch myself creating the story and reframing it into a question. I really want to understand, and if I can't ask my people why they have Trump stickers, who could I ask?

In the store or behind the wheel of the car, I talk to myself when someone's driving in a way I say is bad. "I don't know what's going on with this person, so get over yourself and just drive." And, I notice a change, not so much in others as in myself. I still post what I see as injustice on Facebook, though not to judge. Instead, because I know a lot of people who can benefit from this. I don't let it rip me up anymore. That's a big shift for me. Breathing helps me get to this point.

I continue to return to my people; they are my medicine. There's another wedding soon. Another nephew marrying a white Catholic girl from a tobacco farm. The potential for stories is good. And then I look at the most recent wedding picture of me and my husband with our daughter and Jasmine, my blue-eyed, blonde-haired niece.

My sister told me, "Jasmine has decided that you've adopted her."

To which I replied, "Perfect."

She's my niece and the flower girl at my wedding. I choose to love my people.

At the moment you realize you have chosen upset (perhaps reminded by one of the five symptoms that knock to wake you up), and after you've made that decision to breathe deeply, take a moment to ask what the phenomena are that brought you to this place. Ask yourself if there is lore or history that you have assumed as fact. Some stories graduate to certitudes we can wear like earned badges on a Girl Scout sash. As the middle child, I grew up lost in the shuffle. Or, as the oldest child, my folks had unreasonable expectations for me, while my younger brother got away with murder. My boss doesn't respect me because I'm a woman. I'm an introvert, extrovert, intellectual, pathological optimist, hopeless romantic, fill-in-the-blank person. Some stories are like flagpoles standing at the center of alienated relationships between mothers and daughters, fathers and sons. They call attention to their audiences, seemingly too daunting to discard. Other lore can be rooted in the past, the deeply heartfelt pain we carry.

We can overlook the fact that every story we choose to live with has a physical impact on those around us. If you choose to push a wheelbarrow of stories into the future, you don't get to complain that so-and-so never changes. Check-in to make sure that the story you are living in your head makes your body feel good. If it doesn't, the people around you might not be feeling so hot either.

John's Story

My wife Sarah was planning her ten-day trip to Ireland with a group of women. She made the trip two years ago, and it was amazing for her. She just loved it to tears. As the trip got closer, I found myself resisting her leaving. My body was tensed as I braced for her departure. I didn't want her to go to Ireland for ten days. We had a lot going on. Our oldest child had just come home from college for a short visit before he was to leave for a summer internship. She was going to miss our middle son's twentieth birthday, and on top of that, she'd be away on Mother's Day. So, I pouted. You see, this had happened before on a previous trip, and she missed Valentine's Day and our oldest son's sixteenth birthday. Not that I'm keeping track or anything...

So now I had a story. Sad John, stuck in "Johnville," left alone, abandoned by my wife. I just couldn't handle it. I'd done it before, but this time I was quick to notice I was going off the rails. I was aware my story was completely disconnected from the actual reality and phenomena.

In that moment, I realized how this story came to be. I was reliving a story about how my mother abandoned me as a child, a story that had nothing to do with Sarah. We'd been married for twenty-five and a half years. Her loyalty was clear; she had never abandoned me. With that realization, I felt my body relax, and intense joy for her filled me. I realized how happy she was going to be for those ten days. That trip was going to spiritually fill her up. Sitting by myself in reflection, I smiled and felt my body open. It was like I was sitting on top of a mountain—peaceful.

We were walking the dog when I shared my experience with her. I'd been telling her I supported the trip, and intellectually I meant it, but my body and head were carrying around that thought of "Bitch, don't go. Stay here." I watched her body shift and her shoulders drop. She started to cry.

Damn. I just witnessed how my story impacts a person. I wouldn't have ever realized it until I saw it with my own eyes. I would have stayed in my own head, complaining about how I'm stuck at home while she's off having fun. I would have spent all this time worrying about me, never understanding the profound effect my little story has on my wife.

After that, I was happy for her. I was happy when I took her to the airport and said goodbye, and I'm still happy for her now. Thank God I was able to change my story, because it's changed me. If I don't hear from her until she gets back in another nine days, that's cool. There's no rope trying to drag her back home.

Have you ever noticed that you can live in the same house with people for a lifetime, and each will have a different version of "the truth?" Remembering those details in life can get so shrouded in story that it warps history and can leave irrevocable damage. Or, like Bob, you can create a story big enough to live in. You get to choose.

My story is that this work, this book, is really important work, especially if you want to live a peaceful life and not repeat the mistakes of the past. I entered parenthood with the expressed goal of not making the same mistakes as my parents, electing instead to make my own mistakes. That was a story big enough for me to acknowledge my frailty as a beginner doing the most important job on the planet, and at the same time acknowledge that my parents made mistakes as we all do. No judgment. Just the facts. You know journalism's Five W's, referred to as the who, what, where, when, and why of the story? In actuality, the "why" is the whole story; the rest is phenomena.

CHAPTER 6

Humans are 60% water.
The rest is story. Like water,
we can't live without it.
We can, however, reframe it.

That's one way of looking at it.

At the end of the day, a story you create can be so entrenched that there is just no room for change. I spent a great deal of time working diligently to prove my perspective about my mom. I argued with family that she was never going to change, that she was borderline diagnosable, and that she resented the close relationship I had with my in-laws. I believed in my story so deeply that I wanted to enjoin others in my rant. And, plenty of people agreed with me, which served as evidence I was right!

There might be someone in your life who you say "pushes your buttons" to spark a specific response from you. Maybe there is a certain someone whose presence arouses one of your five symptoms. Fight or flight can feel like the only options available. However, recalcitrance does not serve well in long-term relationships, and hiding from someone over the course of a lifetime is not easily attainable. Listen to your body when you are in these situations, and you may discover one, or more, of your five symptoms.

Reframing, the ability to see your perspective through a different set of can enable you to create a story big enough to live in. It's a bit like having an out-of-body experience. It allows you to be an observer at the moment, floating with the conversation with no requirement to participate. At the end of the day, Mom was actually a little crazy. Realizing I was not required to respond in kind was a big relief.

Mom, raised in a very affluent Catholic family, was the family rebel. She broke rules about smoking and stashed a frozen guinea pig from biology in her mother's freezer. She was funny as hell. She was asked to leave St. Louis University after sneaking out of the dorm. She eloped and was later persuaded to marry him in the Church, only to end up a very young, divorced, single mother in 1960. She then married an unemployed musician with two children from a previous marriage. After moving three hours away, she started her next life living in a trailer next to a horse farm. She had two more children, started her own business, shuttered the business, married one more time, and died at seventy-seven. That's some of the phenomena.

I was her child, and she let me know it on a regular basis. As the oldest, I was expected to excel. I obliged without objection. I would not be who I am today without her strength, guidance, and belief in me. She didn't like any boy I dated. They were never good enough for me, and never as smart, cute, or kind as I thought they were.

In college, I became engaged to an older man. She threw me out of the house with only the clothes on my back. Later, I fell in love with my opposite. With her encouragement and approval, at twenty-three years of age, I married into a vapid, emotionless relationship. Years later, in my second marriage with two children, her tirades became too troubling. My very young children kept their distance. There were long periods after horrific scenes with slamming doors, throwing things, and cursing where she was banned from her grandchildren and my life. It became an unbreakable cycle—until the day I ended it, and my relationship with her. That's some of my story.

As I write the words all these many years later, my shoulders tense. I can instantly hear and feel that famous slam of a kitchen cabinet in my body. I can call back the first of my five symptoms, the knot (my teacher) in my stomach when I saw her calling my cell phone. Her voice still resonates in my head. There is a physical toll to the pattern of this story, which even with her death, survives the ages through our family lore.

Bring to mind your mother, your mother-in-law, or your crazy aunt or uncle—that person in your life that "sets you off." I'm fairly certain there is a rich set of adjectives—a story—that comes to mind to support your assertions.

Sit back and ask yourself, "What is my story about this person?"

Do you see a pattern in your interactions? Is there a trigger that when pulled can transport you back to your thirteen-year-old self and give you permission to react in a practiced way? As you listen and hear your details, what do you observe in your body? Take a minute to write it down. Document these "vitals" as a doctor does so that you can revisit and explore them. This will lead you to be alive to the patterns of your behavior.

Now, let's see if I can reframe my story about my mother with the following questions.

What is her full name?
My story: *Marilyn Blatterman/Buck/Howard/Burkhart*

What does she love in life?
My story: *Gardening, playing the piano, boating, cooking, decorating, and sewing*

What is she about?
My story: *Getting "it" done through her volunteering and work, writing cookbooks, creating tennis programs, and*

designing wedding dresses. Traveling and adventure, with friends or with me, to foreign countries and New York City. In the seventies, she went to Acapulco where she and her friends met a high-ranking general on the beach and spent the evening in his mansion high on the hill, so the story goes. New challenges. Creating.

What stories do other people tell?
Their stories: *A loyal friend, funny, calm in a crisis, and ever at the ready to help. A force of nature. Creative and smart.*

What was her childhood like?
My story: *Devoutly Catholic with lots of rules. She adored her father, a brilliant chemist. Her mother lived a country club life of leisure filled with golf and bridge, and she always had live-in help. It was not a physically warm house. No pets were allowed. She was raised with a nanny and learned to cook from the staff. They had one meal assigned for each day of the week, and it never varied. She was forced to eat a banana every day. She and her two sisters had a million ways to dispose of them. She played the male roles on stage at her girl's Catholic high school. For some reason, she spent a summer on a chicken farm.*

As you revisit your person using these questions, how has he or she changed? Can you see that you have created a different story than the go-to version that is habit? Reframing is using a large-minded perspective of the whole, in this case, person. Too often, we put the most challenging people in our lives, to whom we often ascribe the greatest ills, in a container that limits our ability to see their history and complexity. He is my father, and she is my mom. Be damned the complete life that brought them to this place and time. We view them with a small mind, practically scripted by our personal history and practiced reactions.

Ask yourself how you feel in your body with this new, large-minded story. Do you feel any tightness, any of your five symptoms, as you visualize this being? Or are you more peaceful in your body with this different version of your story? Will you choose to stay in this version of your story? Because, the other option is to continue being upset with this relationship.

THE PRACTICE

How can you get to a place where you can consistently reframe this relationship to live a life without the upset you create in the presence of this person?

Commit to the story that serves you best. Choose a large mind over a small mind, a story large enough to live a life in. Choose to be at ease in your body, to consciously abandon your practice of being upset in the presence of your person.

Change your language. Use a different word as you repeat your story. Play a game of Mad Libs. When you make your proclamations (e.g., my mother doesn't respect me), change it up. "My mother doesn't google me." It wakes you up. It allows you to see the story you are creating and does so without your personal assignment of blame. Let's face it: we judge ourselves as we are judging this "teacher" we are in a relationship with when the words start to fly. Often, we feel remorse in the moment. If not, we may feel it in the hours and days after the event.

A twist of language can force you to quickly wake up to your certitude. Remember, words are drugs. A simple game of Mad Libs can blast the power of those words into oblivion, leaving you with the ability to choose new words at will.

"My mother doesn't respect me, and I'm sick of hearing that my kids are ungrateful" versus "My mother doesn't suspect me, and I'm sick of hearing my kids are tomatoes."

"My dad is an alcoholic" becomes "My dad is a popsicle."

Change "She's upset because of the cancer" to "She's upset because of love."

I can choose my reaction; I change frustration to curiosity, anger into bewilderment, and fear into compassion.

Ask yourself, "If I were to die today, would this upset be worth it?" This is not a choice that can be sugarcoated. I asked myself this question a million times over the years regarding my mother, and I answered yes more than no. For me, the welfare of my children, my spouse, and finally, myself required that I set boundaries that kept me far from the drama, the cursing, and the yelling.

I flipped the switch and reframed my relationship with my mother just in time. We had our concerns that she was slipping mentally after one of her many moves, this time away from family and back to the East Coast. It was a move of opposition against what she accurately declared—the consensus and organized effort of her three children to stop her.

Listening from afar, things seemed to be getting harried around her latest decision to get this newest home ready for sale and move—again—to a new neighborhood. The phenomenon that concerned me the most was the fact that the Christmas decorations were still up, even though Easter was right around the corner. I agreed to make the pilgrimage to the South Carolina coast to evaluate the situation, explaining to her that she couldn't celebrate the resurrection of Christ and his birth at the same time. I was coming to take down decorations.

Our visit was the most peaceful we had ever had. Perhaps because it was just the two of us. But, more likely, it was because I saw her differently, and I was different myself. I marveled at her talents and her ability to put together yet another home with the flair she was known for. I played the role of observer. I noted but did not comment on the issues she was having with keeping her home, checkbook, cable bill, and credit cards in order.

I let her be my tour guide. When it became clear there were limitations to driving in the dark or rain, I gently stepped in to (literally) take the wheel. I let go of my expectations of her and the story about her need to control life. I also took care of my needs, catering to my diet preferences, doing yoga, and taking runs. I acknowledged her gifts to me, the family, and her community. I did not question her decision to move. I did, however, take copious mental notes to report back to my siblings.

My next visit was my last visit. Less than three months later, I was first on the scene at the hospital where she was spiraling into full-blown dementia. She never came back to us. She was gone in a matter of weeks. I gave her eulogy. Written for her grandchildren, it focused on the gifts she brought to the world and to them. It was written so they could understand that there are many different kinds of stories about their grandmother and that each of them has been uniquely bestowed the gift of one of her many wonderful traits—her musical talent, love of gardening, and creative way with color. I reframed the story about their grandmother to create one I hoped would be big enough for them to live in.

The people we surrender our power to, those who inspire you to feel physically bad or motivate you to drug a whole room with the language of dysentery, are rarely folks who are inconsequential to our lives. That's not to say that strangers can't create harm to those around them or politicians are incapable of drugging us through the airwaves. The vast majority of our societal ills are rooted in stories far too small to accommodate all the lives they touch. Yet, even then, in the face of the most heinous of situations, there is hope.

The news recently showed a young man testifying at the sentencing of a police officer. He requested permission from the judge to hug his brother's murderer. As I watched the two embrace, my body became peaceful. Our problems—whether people, places, or things—are our teachers. At the Thanksgiving table, in the classroom, or the boardroom, there is no story so important that it doesn't deserve a happier ending. Especially if it is a story about political beliefs, which over the past several years has become divisive for many families and friends, generating enormous suffering. Reframing offers that opportunity to smooth the edges. Challenge yourself to be curious about what you believe to be outrageous instead of being dogmatic in your response. And if all else fails, surrender to a game of Mad Libs in your head.

CHAPTER 7

Making a request versus a demand.

The ability to make a request instead of demanding action from someone seems like such a simple thing. Yet, at its core, upset is often caused due to our desire to change something or someone. In the beginning of the book, when we learned about breathing, I spoke of that moment when you've hit your limit. *When the kids are yelling in the back seat of the car or the person in your meeting is telling you, again, why something just won't work. When you've walked in the house after a long day, and there are shoes and coats all over the entry hall, and the kitchen dishes are still in the sink. The television is blaring in the family room, but no one is watching it. The dog, or maybe it was the cat, has thrown up on the floor.*

At that split second before you spewed your upset into the mix, I asked that you take four deep breaths to release your body tension. This is done to ease mental and physical suffering, giving you the opportunity to reframe and re-cross the threshold, laying at bay the suffering your verbal whiplash was about to deliver. What if there was a way to eliminate the mess inside the door before you crossed the threshold?

It sounds crazy, but it is possible (except for the involuntary animal disgorge, of course). I'm not naïve. I know you've told the kids a hundred times to turn off the television and the lights when they leave a room. Child One was likely assigned dish duty for the week. Everyone knows coats belong in the closet on hangers, so you shouldn't even have to mention it.

Earlier in the day, you had that conversation at work about missing deadlines with your team for the fourth time. It's beginning to seem as though the project will never be complete. And that argument in the car this morning might have been the result of someone forgetting something you needed, but even you can't quite remember the details at the time.

We make requests of people all day long. Some are met, and many are not. So, we spend the day constantly wanting things to be different, complete, and better, making up stories about why they aren't. This generates upset for you, your employees, your colleagues, and your family as you wonder why the little things bedevil us the most.

Too often, our solution is to take on the task ourselves…at a price. Fold the laundry and empty the dishwasher one too many times, and the resentment starts to build. You may take on that undone assignment at work for fear you might be rejected if you ask your colleagues for help again. Or you may just avoid that employee who can't seem to get the job done the way you want it done and risk the health of the team and the isolation of one of its members. What if you aren't making a request at all? What if you have been making demands all along? They are two very different things.

A demand is nonnegotiable. Child One may not run into the street, period. Homework must be completed by its deadline. Regular school attendance is required, aside from excused absences. Payroll must be completed every two weeks. Our business terms require delivery in thirty days. This sounds like a reasonable way to manage everyday life, except for the fact we are not machines. Our success will be gravely limited if we are forced to manage the complexity of our schedules and the multiple demands on our plates. Remember, we are humans who need to breathe with the ability to negotiate terms.

A request is negotiable. A request acknowledges there are at least two parties engaged and committed to successful action. A request allows one party to decline, to say, "No, I can't do that." If you are asking someone to do something and can't accept a "no," you are making a demand. If you make demands all day long (and many of us do), you'll have a lot of unhappy people on your hands who can't successfully meet deadlines. Productivity will go down. Clients will complain that deadlines are being missed. Overusing demands stifles creativity, slows problem-solving, forces everyone into a scramble to please, and creates upset.

Think about the environment you create at home when you constantly demand Child One, Child Two, and your spouse to execute his or her chores. How often are you satisfied with the results? Laundry is left in the dryer. Dishes from the sink have been moved to the dishwasher. The dirty pots and pans are still on the stove, and the counters haven't been wiped down. Coats are tossed onto the closet floor. The trashcan is still at the bottom of the driveway. It's nine o'clock in the evening, and homework isn't done.

These demands don't seem to be working out well for anyone, especially for you, who then walks around in frustration with five symptoms flaring. Your chest is heaving for breath, only attainable from that belly. There is a story brewing in the background about a lack of respect. Upset seems far, far away from being optional.

THE PRACTICE

Making an effective request is a skill that requires using a clearly-defined process that enables uniform participation.

Create a peaceful request. The first rule about making a request is to not do so when you are upset. At its core, upset is most often the result of an unmet request. The change, action, or terms you want have not been met. You become upset and start that cycle of not breathing, telling a story, and experiencing your five symptoms. Before you make a request, do a body check-in.

Define your request with clarity. Exactly what is it you want? What is it that is missing? Maybe it's not the mess at home, maybe it's a mess at work. Maybe it's both. It's not complicated, but it does require internal observation. The doors into our home and work are thresholds into our lives. We can use them for more than gaining entry. We know that upset is contagious. Are you sneezing when you walk across the threshold into your home? Is there an unresolved issue or an unmet request at work that is causing upset?

And in the reverse, issues that occur at home and even on the way to work can impact everyone in your path. The car that cut you off, the argument over unwashed dishes, or past upsets you haven't chosen to let go of? You'll need to be clear about what it is you want in order to make an effective request.

What you define as a mess might not meet someone else's definition of a mess. As many of us know, there are people who are very comfortable living out of a pile of clean or dirty laundry on their floor. And there are people who do not feel a need to file the papers on their desks and people who are not compelled to participate on every email string. Be as specific and complete as you can when making a request.

Clarify the conditions of success—the who, what, where, and when. Determine who the request is specifically for. Is it the entire sales team or the manager of the team? Specifically define what the request is. Does it matter where this work happens? If so, specify that. When is the request due? How is the finished product to look? How is it to be delivered, to whom, and in what format? If you make no assumptions, you leave less room for error and misunderstanding. Cleaning the kitchen means dishes go in the dishwasher, pots and pans are washed and put away, and the counters and table are wiped down. It's not done when you go to bed at ten o'clock? Then you failed to include that term in your request.

Ensure commitment to the conversation. There is art in the language of making a request. Before you make your request, ensure both the speaker and listener are committed to the conversation. I have a dear friend who once told me that multitasking means you are paying more attention to one thing over another. These days we overcommit our attention to tasks and are constantly bombarded by electronic conversation—email, texts, headphones, and watches. Constant stimuli are distracting. You wouldn't negotiate a pay raise and monitor your phone at the same time.

Making an effective request without the full attention of both parties could be equally risky. The constant use of "will you do this for me?" can be lost on the ear. The language of a well-articulated request is alive and requires listening and—equally important—participation.

"I request (who) you, James, (what) complete the sales report (when) by five working days before the end of every month for the eastern regional offices. I need them (where) delivered to me in hard copy and by email."

And here is the really important part of the request (and, frankly, this part is not optional):

"Do you accept, decline, or counteroffer?"

The use of this interestingly worded question will support you in the goal of achieving total engagement. It will ensure the full attention of your listeners, who are now empowered to negotiate your request versus offering an enthusiastic or lackluster "yes" and moving on down the hall or skulking up the stairs. The offer to accept, decline, or counteroffer requires the full attention of both parties to the conversation. This is why neither of you can afford to be distracted by phones. This is not a casual conversation in the hallway.

James can accept the terms and conditions of your request, alerting the applause meter in your head to celebrate. Or James can say, "No, I decline the request." A request can be declined; a demand cannot. Should James say no, you must be prepared to move on to the next available person to fulfill your request.

James can also make a counteroffer. His current timeline for obtaining updates to the revenue forecast from his sales team doesn't allow sufficient time to complete the report by the date required in your request. He counteroffers by saying he can fulfill the request by the last day of each month.

You can negotiate his proposed terms, or you can decline his offer. If you decline to negotiate, you're stuck. Now, you are making a demand, one that by logical standards appears to be unachievable. If you negotiate, you can let James know the Board of Directors is insisting on monthly sales reports. The two of you can review the calendar and determine how best to get the Board the information they need, all the while ensuring James' sales team's efforts are reported accurately and in a jointly-agreed timeline manner. A successful negotiation means everyone's concerns are acknowledged.

What if it doesn't work? What if I negotiate the terms, and we have a clear and documented understanding, only for the deadline to be missed? That's when you declare a breakdown. Clearly, something went wrong. The question is "What went wrong?"

Were your conditions of satisfaction clear? Was there ample opportunity for James to decline? Could it be there is a story or expectation that any hint of declining could result in rejection? Regardless, declare a breakdown and renegotiate those terms now. If you choose not to renegotiate, you will most likely resort to making a demand, if not of James, then of the next person on your list. Just think of all the goodwill that you would burn. Disregarding the concerns of one of your managers has a ripple effect. You just sneezed on the entire sales team!

There is a fun exercise that illustrates how quickly we feel the effect of a request. Two people sit across from each other. Person A is assigned to ask Person B for a glass of water. Person B is told to say "no" to the request, no matter what, for one minute. The roles are reversed, and Person A is told to deny Person B's request for one minute. The response can be highly amusing. Cajoling, sweet talking, physically feeling tightness in the chest, maybe growing more and more frustrated as you plead, even beg, the person next to you who sits stoically saying, "Nope, no water for you!"

When the roles flip, you'll find yourself trying to outthink your partner, and the only change is a new kind of frustration in not being able to just get the bloody water for him or her. The exercise demonstrates that you will physically respond in some very obvious ways to a simple request of less than ten words. Imagine the stomach flips, tense shoulders, and set jaws around a superior's request for something of substance.

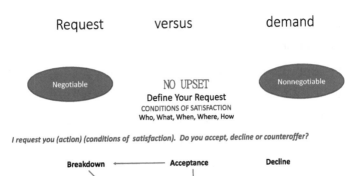

Request   versus   demand

Negotiable   NO UPSET   Nonnegotiable

Define Your Request
CONDITIONS OF SATISFACTION
Who, What, When, Where, How

I request you (action) (conditions of satisfaction). Do you accept, decline or counteroffer?

Breakdown ← **Acceptance**   **Decline**

Renegotiate → **APPLAUSE**

Learning to consistently make a request instead of a demand is a summation of how to use language in its most effective form. It requires you to enter the conversation without any upset so that you can choose words that do not harm. There is no room for story when you are determining the conditions for satisfaction. No one is asking why in this scenario. And, if a story arises, it is most likely because the request has not been satisfactorily met.

With this breakdown, you now have the ability to quickly reframe the story and stay open to possibilities. Our world is indeed a stage. You can enter stage left or right; there are no closed doors. Using this tool with its unique language and carefully designed method allows for a more peaceful path in our daily lives.

PART III

**Do not abdicate your power
in the time you have on Earth.
Engineer your day to effectively
use the gifts you've been given.**

CHAPTER 8

Listening is not a passive exercise.

I like to think I'm a really good friend. I like to think I tend to my friends' hearts as well as I do their stomachs, feeding them the love I feel for them. I like to think that I deeply listen to their dreams and desires with a heart that does not judge. That said, I like to fix things. Occasionally, that works well. One day, out of the blue, my son called me to talk about work. Things were unsettled. The way he was being compensated was shifting; retirements were going to impact who he reported to. He didn't ask for advice, and yet it became clear to me (meaning I created a story) that he was looking for guidance.

We walked through his options. We talked about ways to communicate, and to whom. I can report that all worked out well, and he navigated his interests quite successfully. I was able to help. Yay for me, for him, and the universe! That said, not everyone wants things to be fixed, needs advice, or calls upon me for my wisdom. No one is better at reminding me of that than my beautiful, smart, and feisty daughter, with whom I speak daily.

She calls at least once a week just to vent about work. She is relatively new to the professional world and spends the best hours of her day with strangers, finding her way through the Swiss cheese of the processes, values, and morals of project management. Searching for her place and ability to do good work, she expresses her frustrations and wonderment at the inefficiencies of humans and the struggles of the workplace.

I am older, wiser, and more versed in these things. I can point to the value in these experiences and help her sort through what is important and what can be ignored. I can help her navigate and be more at ease, reducing the upset. She, however, doesn't want one bit of any of this. She just needs me to listen. And when I don't, electing instead for 'fix it' mode, I hear about it! Usually, she uses words that no mom wants to hear from her darling daughter, which then prompts me to hang up on her. Damn. When am I going to learn to keep my mouth shut and just listen?

We are busy people with many things to do. Demands on our time seem to always exceed the supply. It's a wonderful feeling on a Friday after work to spend time and enjoy great conversations with friends or family over a leisurely dinner.

Ask yourself, "Is anyone really listening? How am I hearing the story about today's events? Am I distracted? Are the kids interrupting? Or better yet, are my own thoughts interrupting how I can truly hear what my companion is sharing?"

Perhaps you are listening, and you find yourself on the edge of your seat eagerly awaiting the moment you can offer your own perspective, solve the problem, and then launch into your own tale of the day.

Listening is really a gift—one that we can thoughtfully bestow on the speaker right in front of us at no cost. Have you ever asked someone to listen to you? It's not a request that sounds rational. It's as though listening is the most natural event in the world, second only to breathing (which we now know requires lots of practice), so there's no reason to specify your need for it.

We become lazy in our listening. Imagine your relationship with your spouse if you listened to him or her relay the day's events with the same attention you held for the music of your favorite artist, the play you just saw, or the replay of Kanye West's conversation with the president. How would you feel if your best friend sat beside you and just listened, without judgment or interruption, asking questions that caused you to pause in reflection? Like the other skills in this book, listening can be developed and practiced.

Can you listen as though your life depends upon it? Because it might. Google "doctor and listening," and you'll get a running list of hits on how to talk to your doctor so he or she hears you. It's a big problem in our healthcare system. We consider it the job of the practitioner to take in every important detail we share so that he or she can make the very best recommendations for our health. We have every reason to believe the doctor's listening is paramount to our well-being.

My kids' pediatrician used to start every visit with, "Tell me what's going on, Mom."

I felt my opinion was valued, educated, and relevant. It is indeed a big hurdle in our healthcare system. If you've ever been at the doctor's office with a loved one who has received a serious diagnosis, you know how hard it can be for that person to take in all the information being relayed. As the third person in the room, you now have two jobs of equal importance. The first is to ensure that the physician is hearing your mom, dad, husband, or wife. Then, you must also listen with rapt attention on behalf of your loved one to ensure every treatment detail can be attended to. In this, there is no room for error.

I think it's important to note that nowhere in this scenario is the doctor's current state of mind under consideration. When you have a sick child in your arms, or you or a loved one is in pain, the last thing you are worried about is your doctor's welfare. That said, a check-in with him or her could go a long way in interrupting the autopilot setting in the normality of a workday. It could be even as simple as asking, "Is your day going well?" We are all doing the best we can to be the best we can.

Imagine a world where every patient believed they were being heard. Imagine a world where you were being heard. Now, imagine a world where you were a practiced listener. What would that sound like?

Several years ago, I decided to leave my job of almost ten years. The timing wasn't great. We were in the throes of a recession, and I knew it would be tight on our finances. I have never had issues with job security and was extremely confident it would work out for the best. I sat with my husband and walked him through my thinking, explaining why I thought it was a good decision. I felt great. Making the decision at that time allowed me to tell the board at an in-person meeting scheduled just before the last annual conference I would manage.

I packed for what would be almost a three-week trip with two conferences, a board meeting, and a small bit of R&R. Along the way, I tried to reach my husband on a daily basis with no luck. He took none of my calls. When catching up with the kids, I would gently ask how Dad was. Everything seemed fine except for his refusal to talk to me. On the eve of my board meeting and announcement of my departure, we finally talked. It quickly became clear that he was extremely concerned about me quitting the job.

"We talked about this," I replied.

"I was listening," he responded.

The ways we distract ourselves when we've been asked to listen are so varied. In meetings, we multitask. We simply pay less attention to what is being said than the phone in our hands. Or perhaps we listen partially, feeling the words flowing by. We pick up the relevant pieces that impact the most important issue—me—leaving the rest to drift away.

Sometimes, I listen in complete opposition to what is being said. These days that happens when I watch the news. Occasionally, I'm listening because I'm in agreement. Each example points to being judgmental. I find it feels better to listen with a degree of ambivalence. I like to filter the information I'm receiving without judgment and be curious about the content and its veracity versus assigning right and wrong. You can actually design the way you listen. Just as you can make a choice to be a storyteller at the dinner table, you can elect to be an attentive listener. There is great power in listening. So how can we practice that?

THE PRACTICE

Choose how you listen. In general, our societal norms point us toward polite listeners. Effective listening requires more than that, though. Effective listening requires engagement and effort. You can commit to not interrupting, and you can definitely commit to not changing the subject—unless, of course, there is a situation that warrants such a drastic measure. There's no need to allow a conversation that ruins the surprise party. There is nothing casual about effective listening, and the rewards can be life-changing.

Be the empty space for the other person to hear his or her voice. My best friend has been on quite the journey for the past few years. Central to her core is her relationship with her daughter. Once an adorable ballerina, she's now a fierce warrior in our armed services and recently engaged to be married. Imagine the emotion this amazing mom, wife, and friend brings to our conversations. The feelings range from deep love, continual worry, frustration, joy, and, in some ways, loss because the child she brought into this world is literally moving on and away.

She is my best teacher when it comes to listening. By giving her the space to hear her own voice, we can speak to the things that make a difference to her, her values, and her future with her daughter and new son-in-law. These are conversations that make a difference for her and her daughter and for me as our friendship continues to deepen and grow. I've known her for twenty-six years, and every year, I grow to know her more deeply. Everyone needs the space to hear their own voice and reflect. As the listener, your obligation in this practice is to be curious.

Be curious. Have you ever been in a conversation where a turn of phrase catches you off guard? Or maybe you were hooked on a peculiar use of a word. Maybe you were confused by some detail you just heard? Instead of asking a question, you elect to be a passive listener and let the conversation continue uninterrupted. You let the opportunity to learn more about whatever concern or possibility might exist with deeper conversation. Even after all these years, I'm left wondering why my mother was sent off to work on a chicken farm for the summer. I wish I had asked more questions. I would love to know if she wanted to go. What was that like for her? Did she learn some lifelong lesson? All I know for sure is that it happened, and it stank, literally. As a young child, I did not express my curiosity.

My best friend uses military terminology that means something totally different to me. What if you interjected a question into the story? If I don't ask her what those words mean, I could be quickly lost in our conversation. I could be forced to start the conversation over or let it pass and move on to the next part of the story. If you ever watch lawyers questioning a witness during an investigation, you'll often hear the phrase, "What do you mean by (insert words)?" Be bold enough to pause and create an interruption that will clarify the conversation.

A co-worker is telling you a story about editing a document being produced by her team. She comments, "David would judge me if I found an error in his work." You wonder what it would mean to be judged by David but leave the question unasked. As the story continues, you find yourself fixated on the unasked question. *David must have a great deal of power over her. So much so that it's keeping her from doing her job. Maybe it's because she's a woman.*

What would have happened if you had been curious to ask what it meant when she said David would judge her? Specifically, calling on her to reflect on a particular choice of words offers an opportunity for clarity on your friend's part. It lets her examine her assertion and its impact. Perhaps there is upset around this issue, one that she says leaves her feeling anxious. When you ask what that means, she says that her jaw tightens and her shoulders rise. Or you can stay silent, elect to create your own story, judge David, and define her upset for her. She won't have the benefit of reflection if your curiosity stays silent.

Listen without an agenda, without judgment, and without planning your responses. I go back to my daughter. Can I just be on the phone for the sake of her literally speaking everything she has held inside for the day's last nine hours? Can I simply observe and stop myself from adding my two cents to solve a problem I've defined for her? Can I prevent myself from working to fix something? Can I make it a practice to ask her what she needs? Now, she is wise enough to ask me for my listening, a clear sign I'm to leave my stories off to the side.

Offer the speaker your attention for the benefit of making a decision or to clarify options. Essentially, we are forced to listen. Many of us are on the phone, in meetings, or working with people all day. These situations require us to listen. Sometimes you can skate by with lazy listening if you aren't the one on the hook for making a decision. That said, there are many times when the failure to give the speaker your attention can cripple or compromise the ability to understand the options and make a really good decision.

I have managed countless board meetings. The governing rules of a board declare there be an agenda, one that is subject to board approval. If you need time for people to just be heard, a board meeting is not the place. What it does mean is that you need a process or—even better—a culture to ensure full engagement. Information must be shared ahead of time to allow for preparation. The agenda needs to note the expectations for each item.

Simply identifying what is a report versus what will require discussion and action sets the stage for effective communication. An associated timeline offers guideposts to ensure adequate time for input. In my head, I remind myself that no point of view is more or less important, even if it feels uninformed to me. We are equals at the table and unified in our overarching objectives. Board agendas are tidy and generally move smoothly. We are effective listeners gathered to clarify our options and make decisions. If only life outside the boardroom offered such clarity.

If you've had the pleasure of supporting your children in their journey to select a college, you will understand the importance and challenge of listening for the benefit of making a decision. I watched in awe (and slight disbelief) as my children stepped on a college campus for the first time, only to determine like and dislike in what seemed an instant. It starts with the tour guide. The power of one person out of thousands of students, faculty, and staff to sway my kid for or against an institution of higher learning seemed irrational at best.

I am not alone. I've spoken with parent after parent who has had this experience. It forced me into a new way of listening to my children because asking "why" they didn't like a school wasn't very revealing. The answer to "why" is, of course, a made-up story. There was no phenomena to evaluate. And yet, these impressions are real, significant, and relevant to the decision. Choosing the first home away from home, the foundation for launching into this version of adulthood and all its trappings, had to be based on something more than an ill-defined process of elimination. I was determined to question in a way that enabled us to progress.

First, I asked myself why I bothered to argue with the opinion. It's not mine to own, and it was pointless to fight. I elected to reframe my story. I decided if I couldn't be successful in getting past my own judgments regarding their opinions—or better—asking the right questions to elicit thoughtful conversation, we were never going to get anywhere in one of the most important and expensive decisions we would make together.

It took time, but after more practice (meaning more school visits), I began to discover some themes. Language. It wasn't just the mechanics of our tour guide's speech and the specific words chosen, though that seemed relevant; it was also the resonance of his or her communication with the group and my kid. The peer-to-peer connection versus a parent-to-student relationship seemed to jump off the page. That insight came from being an observer and listening to the students and their relationship with our guide versus putting myself in college shoes again and reliving my days. It looked a bit like dating, only taking a minute to see if there was a fit. This small window seemed limited in its ability to enable a final decision. However, it was a mirror to the next theme I discovered.

Culture. These tours served as an authentic interpretation of campus life. I was struck by how some schools attended to the ways students move on campuses. Some made permanent the natural crisscross of human traffic across campus lawns, while others seemed oblivious and assumed all would adapt to sidewalks demanding right-angle foot traffic. It was clear that some schools were spending enormous sums of money to modernize the campus in a way they believed fit this generation's needs. Others relished traditional architecture, which seemed to be designed to showcase legacy. Dartmouth didn't even bother to do a tour of their dorms. My daughter failed to see the significance of that.

You can't fake diversity well, a fact that bounced off the page for my city-raised kids. Large outdoor spaces with students gathered in play or study versus a compact array of discordant architecture seemed to evoke two very different responses. Comments like weird and quirky seemed to reflect a regional affectation of style and dress.

Oddly, even on very large campuses, students seemed to dress alike. And finally, what I call mission and vision, became a central issue. A tour guide who connected the school's purposes with the land and community it resided in captured my son's attention and interest in the environment. A guide who spoke of the intellectual opportunities to discover how to contribute to the world would push the school higher up on my daughter's list.

I had lots of opportunities to practice listening. Ohio versus New Hampshire versus Vermont versus Rhode Island and more. All the schools and cities were evaluated against Washington, DC, where they grew up. Some of the best listening I've ever had the opportunity to enjoy happened on those campuses and during the drives, especially when the applications were completed and when the decisions were made.

Kids and colleagues give us some of our best opportunities to be solid listeners. Why? We can frame our listening around purpose. We have intentions when it comes to raising our children. And these conversations with our children have a lasting impact.

There were many kitchen table conversations about my biological father after that first one at age eleven. I was grateful when my adoptive father began to share the story. It filled in some of the blanks. It shed light on the times I would walk into a room as a child and silence a conversation I intuitively understood was about me, even at a very young age.

I was a senior in high school when I first spoke with my biological father on the phone. He had an uncanny ability to call when my parents were out. He sent me pictures. I now understood my three parents had been having a conversation about me all along. My curiosity grew, and the parents I grew up with listened carefully as I moved through my on-and-off decisions to meet him. And though I had not yet met him, Dad gently asked if I would like my real father to walk me down the aisle at my wedding to my first husband. Incredulous, I recovered my composure. I hugged him tight and let him know he was my real father.

When I was finally ready, I went to Mom, who agreed to track my biological father down one last time. During the conversation with the man who was my mirror image, I listened to the stories that clarified where I came from. Then, I sat with my parents at the kitchen table once again.

"I am so grateful that you chose to raise me as your daughter," I told my dad. "My life would have turned out so differently."

Becoming emotional, Dad had to leave the table. I'm fairly certain as we traveled through the rest of his life together, he knew he was the only father I ever needed or wanted.

Looking back, this could have gone so differently. For years, my parents listened to my questions and coped with me changing my mind about meeting this man. I often wondered, out loud, why the only father I had known since the age of three didn't adopt me until I was in the fifth grade. The two of them could have slammed doors shut or forced me into action I was not ready for. I still marvel at the patience they brought to this topic. They had an uncanny ability to listen to a young, curious child and leave their stories of hurt on the curb. They did not judge me but instead found a way to meet me and my curiosity as it ebbed and waned through adolescence. Leaving any expectations to the side, they listened deeply as I struggled to make that decision to meet my biological father, not over a period of days but years. Perhaps they understood their listening mattered because my life, and our life together, depended on it.

And finally, don't be afraid to ask for listening. Just as there is power in listening, there is power in asking to be listened to. I'm not talking about the occasional "You never listen to me!" or the "Will you just listen this once!" commentary. First, don't take it for granted that you are being listened to. If there is any doubt or if it is essential to you, ask for it. Awkward? Perhaps. But the stakes can be high. Try on the words "May I have your listening?" It's a turn of phrase that will capture their attention. It's a wake-up, a hiccup that causes eyes to fall away from phones.

Sure, there are other ways to phrase such a request. The funny thing about them is that they often have their own triggers. "We need to talk" can land in my body like the slamming of truck brakes. Just writing it sets my spine straighter. So why not try something new? Turn that noun into a verb and see if the conversation can be one of curiosity and reflection, not judgment. Explore possibilities and solutions by starting out with effective listening.

CHAPTER 9

Hate having a bad day? Design each day by defining your mood.

On one hand, it makes sense that mood is defined as a temporary state of mind or feeling. After all, whoever could maintain the same mood for an entire day? And, there are far too many instances where, had I stayed in the same mood all day, it would have been highly detrimental to everyone around me. It's like when you have that feeling that you just can't create, concoct, solve, or share one more thing, idea, or piece of advice. Perhaps there are times when you feel disconnected and exhausted.

What the hell is that anyway? Perhaps it's definition two of mood, which, according to Oxford, is "an angry, irritable, or sullen state of mind." That seems very familiar. We act as though mood is something that happens *to* us, using terms like "I woke up on the wrong side of the bed." Is there really a wrong side of the bed on which to start my day? What would life be like if I could design my mood for the day and maintain that outlook despite life's certain interruptions?

We've all been in a room with someone in a bad mood. It's as contagious as any cold or flu, perhaps more so. Essentially, "being in a mood" is no different than using language as a drug. It's just silent. Being in the room with someone who is smiling, making eye contact, and engaging in conversation is equally contagious. These moods need not be accidental. They are not things that happen to you unless you cede your power. There is a third option, a choice to design your mood to induce your own state of mind.

It's routine to have a schedule—an alarm to wake us, a dog to walk, coffee to consume, and a calendar to guide the day. Some practices we take for granted; others we deem essential to a productive day. Adding to the to-do list is common practice. So why not add two minutes to set an intention (perhaps while engaging in the morning ritual of brushing your teeth) to design your mood for the day? Be your own "mood music."

Before the opportunity to react shows up, start your day by taking ownership of your mood. The possibilities far exceed the boundaries of good or bad mood. You can choose peaceful, creative, loving, observant, or joyful. Determined, diligent, and open are other options. Find a mood that resonates in your body at that moment on that day, and it will bring with it the same power as the upset each of us will no doubt be grappling with several times over the course of the next twenty-four hours. Therein lies the real work—learning how to recover and maintain our designed mood in the face of life's extraordinary and ordinary events and our tendency to react in the moment.

I used to design my daily mood while walking my dogs in the quiet of the morning. The symbiotic relationship of my five senses, combined with the stillness of the day's start, flowed through my body and resulted in what I chose to define as peaceful. Sans dogs, I will often lay in bed and take a couple of moments to design my mood for the day. Ninety percent of the time, my choice is peaceful. If I forget to design, I'll make room for it after my feet hit the floor. And just to be absolutely clear, ninety percent of the time, I will lose that mood at least once in the first three hours of the day.

We live in a world constantly bombarding us with news, events, and information that in itself can be jarring. And too often, it is presented in a way specifically designed to jolt the senses into reaction. Our bodies are seemingly hardwired to react. The work becomes learning how to notice that shift in my body when I am angered, startled, or even horrified so I can then reframe and return to that peaceful mood.

THE PRACTICE

There are those of us, mostly former Girl Scouts, who remember the "stop, drop, and roll" drill in the event you catch on fire. I'm quite certain that if I ever did catch on fire, I would literally stop moving to drop to the ground and roll those flames away. Sadly, today's children are being schooled in potentially life-saving active shooter drills. It's a physical disruption for the sake of saving lives. The practice of designing and maintaining my mood is similar in intention if not design. I can train to respond to the inevitable interruption of my peaceful body state. What I need to learn are the signals (some subtle, some not so subtle) from my body alerting me to the highjacking of my artfully-designed, daily practice.

Set your mood. Create a mood that matters to you. Change it every day or every week. Keep the same mood for a lifetime. Combine all the above if you want. The point is to identify the way you want to be as you walk through your day. Name it and allow yourself the luxury of feeling that mood in your body. None of those five symptoms can live in the mood you have designed. Your breath is slow and deep in your belly. Life is good in this moment, even peaceful. This is how you are choosing to feel and be for the day.

Remember, you picked a mood! Begin with check-ins—not just one, but periodically through the day.

- Place sticky notes with your word on the bathroom mirror, the car dashboard, your office coffee mug, or anywhere your eye routinely travels to remind you of your intention.

- Use your screen saver to bounce your mood choice across your computer screen.

- Set an alarm on your phone or watch. Sometimes, a unique and unexpected buzz is the best way to awaken that morning promise to be [insert mood] for the day.

- Phone a friend. Enlist a friend or colleague to check in with a quick text and ask, "What is your mood?"

- Move a ring or a watch to a different hand. It will feel unsettling. It is physically disrupting and will remind you of the intention you set for today's mood.

Check in with your body. Pick times during the day to do a quick body scan. Have you generated any familiar physical attributes? Are your shoulders raised? Is your throat tight? Do you feel any of your five symptoms need tending to? With this practice, you are training yourself to wake up from the daily doldrums. You are setting alarms to remind you that taking care of the day and the people in your day requires being awake, actively designing each step instead of assuming there are forces dictating the way things will be.

Push the reset button. How do you feel when you are having a bad day? Perhaps you created a story that drove you to conclude it is bad. Maybe you find yourself upset, jaw clenched, with the potential for your five symptoms to pop into your awareness. My email isn't working, the dog ate my ChapStick (again), and my hair dryer blew up...I'm having a bad day.

It's possible you will sneeze on people as you walk through this "bad" day. You could be Sara, who walked by me in the hall without speaking, leaving me to wonder if I had somehow offended her. You could be my boss, barking orders disguised as a request. You can choose otherwise. Stop, drop your shoulders, and let that upset roll off your back. Acknowledge there are adversities in life. Bummer. Make an agreement to recommit to the mood you designed for the day. Breathe into that mood and redesign how you will walk and talk throughout the remainder of your day (or at least until the next emotion, event, or word takes you off course). Repeat.

Designing your mood speaks to your intention for the day or week. Over time, you will find it serves as a declaration of how you want to be in the world. We take on this work for ourselves and our health. The power of the work grows in its authenticity as you observe the impact of what appear to be small changes—small changes that, in reality, have a serious impact on your biochemistry. You are creating a declaration for the sake of the people for whom it makes a difference. You have the power to hold the space for upset, anger, sadness, and pain while maintaining your mood. We can be peaceful in upset.

Impossible, you say? As noted, there will be times when each of us becomes upset. One morning, I opened my computer to find a dark and mysteriously cracked screen. I had two options. I could freak out, knowing I was going to lose at least three days with my favorite companion no matter what I tried. Or I could move into effective action.

I took several deep breaths, thwarting off that nugget of panic by talking to myself. After grabbing my old computer, I went through the necessary steps of getting it live and hooked to the Cloud. I found the document I needed (this book), and while the tiny gerbils warmed up the wheel in my ancient and slow Mac, I used my phone to pop into the online genius bar to schedule my appointment for a repair.

None of this is ideal, of course. With our amazing access to technology, we carry an expectation that everything can and will work instantaneously. That said, within a matter of fifteen minutes, I found myself up and running, breathing and still peaceful. Did I have a minute where my favorite symptom, the friendly knot in my stomach, woke up? Absolutely. And I'm grateful that I was able to recognize it as the teacher it is and shift back into a calmer and, frankly, more useful person.

In today's world, the ability to maintain a designed intention and/or mood is a life skill we can all benefit from. We have come to rely heavily on professionals who, in a time of crisis, are trained to save lives, and I am deeply grateful for their service in the face of natural disasters, accidents, and domestic and foreign terrorist attacks. I am also deeply aware that in the face of social media, opposition politics, and a 24/7 media cycle, many of us struggle to maintain balance in the face of a different type of crisis.

Race relations, politics, financial security, and fear for a healthy future have indeed improved ratings for the Hallmark Channel and, I suspect, increased gym memberships. However, can one maintain a designed mood of joy in the face of discord? Can peace exist at the Thanksgiving dinner table when politics is tearing families apart? Is it possible to move through the day with brightness and calm and still be fierce in the desire to serve humanity, protect dignity, ensure justice, and represent the causes we believe in? After all, we are all advocates, especially for the people we love. Is there room for anger?

There was a time in my marriage when things were very dark. I was committed to family dinner being an essential part of our routine, and I was dedicated to seeing it through as long as my two children were living in the house. There were years when the kids were little that one cocktail before dinner became two, accompanied by a shared bottle of wine with dinner. A once pleasant ritual grew stale for me as the children got older, more conversant, and engaged. Not so for my spouse who would come home from a highly-stressful teaching environment and medicate his pain through dinner. My upset was palpable as I worked to make a family dinner and maintain an upbeat and interesting dialogue for the kid's sake, hoping to distract them from the nonresponsive person at the end of the table. I could not stay in my designed mood through a meal, and no amount of conversation on the topic with my husband led to change.

The hardest lesson I ever learned from my mentor Bob Duggan was that *everything is perfect just the way it is.*

"How," I asked him, "is it perfect that the father of my children is getting drunk at the dinner table during the week, barely able to converse?"

I remember his eyes hardening a bit as he responded. I felt his sense of urgency and the intention in his words, even though I could not grasp his explanation. It took me years to understand that he meant, in the simplest of terms, that I couldn't change my husband any more than I could stop my plane from being canceled. It is what it is. It is not a thing to be discarded nor a problem to be fixed. Rather, it's something I must be peaceful with if there is any hope of change to be had.

Understanding I could only control my circumstances, in the short term, I elected to leave the dinner table and eat elsewhere. It felt like a poor solution for my kids' well-being. Although, it allowed me to reset my mood and let go of what I wanted to control. It was an illusion to believe I could control the situation. It was insanity to want to fix my husband's imperfections. It was painfully perfect, just the way it was.

I wish I could tell you that I saved my children from years of watching this dysfunction. I did not. Over time, I believe I was able to convey to my children an understanding that one person's choice does not have to adversely affect you. I maintained my sense of curiosity and demonstrated hope for what was possible versus dwelling on what was wrong. Perhaps that is one way of maintaining a peaceful mood in a sea of upset.

Anger did not serve me well in my marriage. As Bob used to say, "You can't make good decisions if you are angry." This does not mean that you must travel through life in a meditative state wearing flower garlands and espousing your love for everyone (although how lovely that would be if we all did). Passion and ferocity are required attributes for those seeking to make effective change. If you care deeply—whether about your children's education, climate change, immigration policy, or violence against minority populations—you will likely find yourself angry. Being effective and being angry don't always work well together. It's that pesky upset that distorts your ability to see possibility and use your practices wisely.

When you choose to be an advocate for change, you must first acknowledge the humanity of the people around you, especially the people you decide are creating the problems. Your inner flower child points to a deep understanding that we are all connected to each other. Be peaceful in your intention to be fierce without causing upset in your own body and spewing hateful language as a drug.

Speak less, teach more, and listen deeply. Avoid sitting in judgment of the opposing viewpoint. When you make your demands, be acutely aware that because they are not negotiable, they will most often never be met. As you request change, be prepared for breakdown. Remember, breakdown is not a failure but an opportunity for more clarity and conversation. Everything is perfect just the way it is. I implore you to design your mood to allow for that.

CHAPTER 10

Acknowledgment

Have you ever wondered why we still watch award shows on television? What is the reason besides enjoying the annual Oscar party and waiting for the inevitable gaff or political commentary? At the end of the night, we will have witnessed a simple act of acknowledgment for the work, skill, talent, and humanity of people. In this case, we acknowledge people we will most likely never know but whose work we have come to love. Think about your physical response to these events. I can become teary watching a beautiful and gracious public thank you delivered on television by a complete stranger.

It's not that we don't seek opportunities to stage our own award shows. There are the multiple award banquets at school that often solicit that same teary response and warm feeling of ease that I call love. The Employee of the Month gets the parking spot. Weight loss competitions at my boot camp highlight hard work and hardened bodies. The list goes on. Some would say we have taken this effort to honor contribution too far. Some may even assert that we have raised a generation where everyone gets a trophy for participation, and children need to learn the lesson of failure.

Yet, most of us feel we never get enough acknowledgment. Maybe this "overindulgence" of participation awards is simply our way of compensating for what is actually missing in the world—genuine recognition of kindness or achievement. We can all benefit from acknowledging that our personal humanity can impact our lives. Ask yourself, "Do I receive enough acknowledgment? Do I give enough acknowledgment?"

Receiving acknowledgment is a challenge for many of us. Can you accept a compliment? Can you really take it in? Do you physically flinch when someone tells you how handsome you are in that blue shirt? Does it leave you feeling uncomfortable, causing you to avert your eyes and maybe cross your arms or look down at your shuffling feet? If I were to look you in the eye and share that I was deeply impressed with your presentation and that it will change the way I approach my work, could you take it in? Or would you be inclined to diminish my offering by waving me off with, "Really, it was nothing"?

Are you acknowledged enough for your efforts? You put in extra hours to make sure everything was perfect for the presentation. You volunteer at the kids' school, raising money to supplement an underfunded public budget. You're the teacher who grades papers well into the night after coaching the debate team after school. You're the janitor who steps into the messes we make and cleans them up wordlessly. You're the boss who forgoes a percentage of his bonus to share it with his team. You're the wife who manages the family finances or the husband who shepherds the kids from homework, to baths, to bed. We are all just human beings, walking down the hall, bumping into each other, and sharing joy, sorrow, anger, or even disbelief as we wander through our day. We are part of a two-legged species restless in a desire to build, create, change, improve, or just survive the day.

What is your story about all this extra stuff you do?

I don't need acknowledgment. It's the least I can do. It's the right thing to do. It's what I do. It's who I am. I'm a giver.

Really? When you genuinely thank the hardworking teacher, janitor, or boss, how do you feel when he or she responds, "Really, it's no big deal"? Do you feel heard? Or does it feel as though your comments have been discarded? Football teams can't win the season with great passing and receiving. This is not a game. The stakes are much higher for us humans.

It is also not an intellectual exercise. When I am acknowledged for an act of kindness, for going beyond someone's expectations, for being generous of heart, or even for the graduation gift I mailed, there is a moment of ease I can allow myself. My face softens, my shoulders drop, and I can breathe deeply into my chest without effort. Sometimes, I can tear up listening and reading these words of appreciation.

My body physically responds to these acts and good medicine words. I prefer to feel this way instead of experiencing the fabulous five symptoms. There are times when I feel unease with words of praise, sloughing off the kindness delivered to me by family, friends, and co-workers. Struggling to make eye contact, I feel tightness in my jaw. Sometimes, I start to sigh, creating a story that my offering is far from remarkable or worthy of "praise." How very rude of me to be so certain in my position that I can easily reject this genuine gift. Without fail, in these moments, I have quit breathing.

All of us need to practice accepting and giving acknowledgment. We number close to eight billion people on this planet, yet we have an innate ability to isolate ourselves physically and emotionally. Spending 5.4 hours on your phone is now "average," an hour of which is consumed by social media. More than half of us spend 2.8 hours a day watching television. Time at the workplace or doing chores at home averages between 10.5 and 11.5 hours per day. The time engaged in real socialization and conversation with other humans averages a mere 38 minutes a day.[1]

---

[1] https://blog.acton.org/archives/109642-7-figures-how-americans-spend-their-time.html

Let's not make this so damned complicated. We humans, when we do bump into each other, each benefit from this practice of acknowledgment. Expressing our gratitude or appreciation for something someone does or gives is another way to enrich our connection to one another and create peace in our bodies.

THE PRACTICE

Receive acknowledgment bravely. There is something that connects acknowledgment to our vulnerability. For me, it shows up in my reticence to accept a compliment. If I agree with you, then I have set myself up to always look good in red lipstick. If I give a good speech, now every presentation must wow the audience. Better to "aw shucks" this whole thing away, so I don't risk embarrassment in the future. Pshaw! Time to pull your big girl panties up! Quit squirming and accept this offer of a gift.

- The next time you are offered a compliment, stop what you are doing and face the person.
- Ask this person to repeat what they said. Or say, "Tell me more about that." The point is to be absolutely certain you understand what it is you are being acknowledged for.
- Drop your shoulders. Open your chest. Practice deep breathing as you actively listen to their response.

- Ask yourself, "Where do I feel this in my body?" Duly note any tightness or discomfort you feel, and then let it go.
- Now you can say, "Thank you."

I am witness to the joy of being on the receiving side of a compliment. And, I have watched the response to my request for more information after I receive the compliment. It is utterly delightful for both parties! We must not let our struggle with knowing what to say, how to say it, and when to say it paralyze us into silence and isolation.

Kindness is a good thing. Accepting a genuine gift of acknowledgment is never the wrong thing to do. We know that because of our body's response. Once you can push aside the awkwardness, you'll notice new sensations. Perhaps, you literally feel lighter on your feet or the furrow in your brow is gone. Maybe you felt the first of your five symptoms disappear when you hadn't even been aware until that very moment it was there. That said, we live in complicated times. Not every compliment is designed by its messenger to be a gift, and the evolving definition of politically correct is leaving land mines in life's path.

If you sense the compliment is offered as anything other than a gift, there is no better way to prevent coercion than to stop what you are doing, look the person straight in the eye, and ask for the statement to be repeated. Ask for clarification while you are deeply breathing. Pay attention to your body, your teacher. If need be, it will let you know to turn heel and walk directly to personnel with your enlightened perspective. This simple practice will empower you in those moments.

Give acknowledgment with intention. We're always looking for a way to give back. We donate time, money, hats, shoes, and socks to demonstrate appreciation for our good fortune. Watching through my big picture window is a central component of my life's view. This is a way I can be kind and helpful and show my gratitude. And yet, we often fail to express our gratitude for some of the smaller things in life. To the person who lets you merge in a line of traffic, a simple wave will do. To the woman who helped you gather the folder of loose papers you dropped on the way into your building, a heartfelt smile would suffice. Even the art of sending a well-articulated thank you is at risk of extinction, which is too bad because it's a really great way to practice acknowledgment.

It's unusual to receive that undersized note in the mail after you have sent the check or gift to the graduate or bride and groom. And, while a well-worded email or text of appreciation is totally acceptable these days, many of our thankful words feel perfunctory. "Thank you for the check, Aunt Karen," in any form of print certainly meets one definition of acknowledgment—"a letter confirming receipt of something." It delights me to know the card was received and money spent instead of having to open my bank statement to see if the check cleared. It also "checks the box" for good manners. It doesn't, however, speak to the gift I bestowed in the content of my letter—my gratitude for her contribution to the world and the happiness she brings into my life. For me, words of gratitude are a drug with a healthy physical response. I can breathe deeply as I listen to them. I can relax the muscles in my neck and shoulders, and I often inadvertently elicit a soft "aww."

Gift acknowledgment daily. Be proactive and organized in your offerings of thank you.

- Choose a moment to acknowledge someone in your life and offer a compliment or words of praise.
- Ask if they will take a moment to carefully listen to something you have to say.
- Speak directly to them. No distractions are allowed.
- Let them know specifically what you are acknowledging them for.
- As you watch the words sink in, ask, "Did you take that in?"
- Breathe deeply and repeat your acknowledgment. "Because it's true!" (Fill in the blanks) "You look____." "Your work inspired me to____." Or perhaps a simple "You just made my day."

If you're feeling this is a bit risky to try, practice on a friend or even a complete stranger. My friend David is a master at making people feel special with these simple words: "You make it look so easy. Thank you for all that you do." I've watched harried waitresses all over the country stop and smile, warmly accepting his praise. It makes a difference, even to me as an observer of this phenomenon. Feel free to appropriate the practice as I have. Gifting gratitude is a sure way to feel better about receiving an acknowledgment. The more I gift, the easier it is to receive. It is a beautiful contagion for the world.

This practice has impacted my life in ways I could not have imagined. I have fallen in love with awards. I love the process of creating an award, writing the criteria, discussing who gets the award, writing the plaque, and most of all, bestowing the award. Honestly, I feel guilty about how much I enjoy all of this acknowledgment.

I write thank you notes with abject delight. And while I certainly do not need to be thanked for a thank you, I admit I do enjoy a bit of back and forth when I get the email in response to one of my written notes of appreciation. I enjoy it because it lets me do one of the things I enjoy most—heap gratitude on a person I greatly appreciate. Honoring the people in my life who choose to make impactful contributions of all kinds is a selfish delight.

Over time, I've come to appreciate that this practice— giving and receiving gratitude or appreciation for something—is bigger than giving an award or writing a thank you note. Recognition of your work, his contribution, your compassion, and her thoughtfulness is acknowledgment on steroids. This is acknowledgment that, as my old camp song goes, will "warm the cockles of your heart and make your life worthwhile."

Why the hell does this matter? No man lives alone on an island. Not even me, even though I live alone and work alone from my home office, all of which I love. I also know that being alone does not complete me. It can't support my ongoing work as a champion for the causes I believe in.

So, I'm constantly on the phone with business partners, family, friends, and people from afar. I travel extensively for business and pleasure, going to weddings, funerals, baby showers, and birthday parties. Life is messy, joyous, tearful, and stressful, and it can leave people feeling alone in a crowded room. All of us are forced to be a part of our human race, like it or not. Yes, acknowledgment can make someone feel good. It can also ensure people are heard, which is a great way to diffuse upset and return to being peaceful.

Sometimes, people just need to be seen and heard. They require acknowledgment that their presence matters. Too many voices are silenced in today's society, usually not for the better. No doubt, there will be times we would rather not listen, whether out of disagreement or because we are short on time. In my experience, when facing a difficult situation, acknowledging the person in front of you is the fastest way to create peace.

Years ago, a member of the association I managed would call on a fairly regular basis, generally to complain. She was the first to tell us we were doing something wrong, and she let us know her thoughts on the "better way." I quickly learned that listening carefully (yes, deeply) to her opinions and thoughts resulted in a lowering of her voice. A conversation could ensue. I could acknowledge her contribution. She continued to call in agitation over the many years I had that job. However, the whole staff learned a valuable lesson about the power of personally acknowledging the humanity of the person on the phone. Acknowledgment can create peace.

A few years ago, ten people (including me) moved into a newly-renovated building, occupying seven units. Three couples and four singles created our own little village. Some of us were starting families, while others were starting new chapters of their lives. We ranged in age from mid-twenties to mid-seventies. We represented cultural differences from other parts of the world. Two of us had life experiences that spanned a total of 130 years. Six were new parents. Little dust-ups can happen over matters that one considers critical, another trivial. Or, in simpler language, one person's discovery of baby snakes in her unit is another resident's personal nightmare.

Simone had lived in Florida, the land of insects and animals. She managed multiple properties before she moved back to the DC area into our pristine, newly-renovated building to be closer to family. From her vantage point, baby snakes were minimally disruptive. The three-member board, who had quietly accepted some of her structural changes, including cutting window screens to allow cats outdoor access, was pushed over the edge of tolerance. As the association president, I wrote the letter to present to Simone. It outlined the requirements we deemed necessary to ensure no pest invasion could occur. I hand-delivered this officially-worded letter, knowing it could be met with resistance, and it was. It was actually thrown to the ground.

People can be hurt by a piece of paper, even before they read it. So, I took the time to acknowledge Simone. I started by telling her that her many years of experience as a homeowner and managing properties gave her a perspective that can only be learned over time. That she and I, as elder residents of the building who were long-term homeowners, had an obligation to help our young neighbors learn the ropes of managing and maintaining their new homes.

I was able to diffuse her upset so she could hear me when I explained that anything that was in her home was in all our homes—that we actually lived in one house. She could look at me and have a conversation about the importance of the issue without a raised voice. She agreed to use our monthly pest service to ensure neither insects nor snakes would become permanent residents of the building.

When you wander into challenging conversations and situations, where stories quickly trigger physical reactions and words can be used as weapons, take time to acknowledge the gifts and humanity of the person in the room. It will create ease instead of suffering.

When my parents were divorcing, my sister and I were married adults. My brother was finishing college. In my experience, we worry (appropriately so) about the health of our young children when a marriage dissolves. What I didn't know was how difficult divorce is for adult children of divorcing parents. It was seemingly impossible to shield us from the mess.

For years, all I had known was their constant fighting and unhappiness. It was illogical to me that my mother would want to stay in her marriage of twenty-five years given my father's relationship with another woman. Her anguish peaked when we gathered for my brother's college graduation. Twenty-five years later, I was extracting myself from my own marriage with a son in college and a daughter in graduate school. I vowed my son's graduation would not be a repeat of my family history. I wanted peace and happiness for our son and the extended family who gathered for this event. And I wanted that peace for every event in our collective future. That meant I needed to go about the process of divorce without creating a mess. Upset is indeed optional.

I drew up our separation agreement, and we signed it. I moved out of the house and agreed to continue the mortgage payments, and we started the conversation about putting the house on the market. We agreed to pay for a mediator, not lawyers, and successfully negotiated our own terms for dividing assets. All told, it personally cost me somewhere around five thousand dollars to get everything done.

I went through the mechanics of this effort by acknowledging my husband—not by thanking him but by demonstrating through my actions and words that we were ending a partnership on equal terms. I did this every time we met, whether during mediation or on the street. I finally put all my cards on the table, and we dealt with the money fairly. He could have dug in his heels, and I could have pitched a fit. Neither happened. I knew it was far more important, for the sake of my kids, that he felt valued, heard, and appreciated. I sat at the mediation table deeply listening to how he felt and what he needed. And when I felt a knot in my stomach, and I did, I sat back in the chair and focused on my breathing. I would not allow myself to lose sight of my belief that his love of our children trumped the fact I did not love him anymore as a spouse. I kept doing this until we finished the process.

By the time we traveled to the graduation, our house was on the market for sale. My (then still) husband shared a suite with me and my daughter at a bed and breakfast. His family joined us for a celebration dinner and my son's graduation. I'm sure the kids would say it wasn't perfect. I'm also fairly certain they were happy we could do it.

I've heard stories over the years about how couples remain friends after a divorce, and now conscious uncoupling is a "thing." I never understood how that was possible, given my history and that of my friends. In my view, conscious uncoupling sounded more like a forty-year marriage where two people sit side by side going silently through life. Now, I know that being peaceful in life requires being peaceful in your body, and that requires practice.

CONCLUSION

Serving Seven Generations

Who benefits from my commitment to these practices?

The turbulence of our times brings to mind Bob teaching the meaning of "oneness" and the power of understanding our connection to one another. He used to tell the story of hearing Thich Nhat Hanh speak.

As we waged the Gulf War, Hanh recited, "I am one with the American people, with George Bush and with Saddam Hussein. I am the bomb that fell from the sky."

One of our practices was to stand in a circle and physically point to another person as we repeated, "I am pointing to myself."

We love the illusion of separateness, believing our own presence on the planet is unrelated to other people's presence. We take comfort in knowing people who do bad things are held accountable, failing to see it is only through compassion and connection that we truly transform our world. A police officer convicted of murder is hugged by the deceased man's brother at sentencing, and we are changed by his act of compassion, connected in that moment to complete strangers. I still use the practice of "pointing to myself" when I am transfixed by one of the frequent horrific reports on television. Reciting those words reminds me I am a piece of what I define as "the problem."

The concept that the richness of life is most fully experienced when we are "one" with one another can be difficult to grasp. Yet, it is represented in virtually all the world's religious traditions. Now, its benefits are documented through modern science. A 2019 survey of almost seventy-five thousand Germans found that the more individuals respected relationships through empathy, a closeness with nature, or "social connectedness," the higher their happiness and life satisfaction scores.

Bob would say, "To live fully means to lose oneself in service of life itself. Life living through you. Not you living life for the sake of yourself."

His practices point to using the wisdom of our bodies to create a peaceful world where we live in service to each other.

It should come as no surprise that we end with one last practice. Consider a time when you have acted only in your own self-interest, selfishly demanding action or diminishing the input of others for your own welfare. How did that resonate in your body? Reflect similarly on an act of charity and kindness you offered. Compare your physical responses.

Despite deeply-felt religious beliefs or an innate understanding of this oneness, we wrestle with a commitment to live a life of service. In our modern culture, we praise individuality. We assert happiness is key and encourage our children to create any life they choose. We eschew the ancient tradition of teaching our children to honor and serve their ancestors—to take action that prepares the world for future generations. We can feel put upon, searching for "me time," having exhausted our bodies with what we call "taking care of others." This most often translates into seeking to control or fix life. And, as Bob said many times, life is seldom ours to control.

It is not that we cast dispersion on the benefits of adopting a generational perspective. In fact, we are madly in love with our generations. Baby Boomers sitting alongside Generation X, the Millennials, and now Generation Z is a common workplace topic. "How," people ask, "can these wildly divergent people all get along and benefit from the experience and enthusiasm of one another?"

I assert this question is too small. Consider the law of the Seven Generations. Spoken in ancient cultures worldwide, it is most known to us through Native American traditions. Some of us have had the fortune to know our great-grandparents. The rest of us are likely to know many of their stories. Some of us have great-grandchildren. I believe all of us have hope for the future we leave to those babies. I choose to live with a sense of responsibility to honor those who brought me to this place and time in life. And I commit to doing the work that will serve future generations.

Years ago, I made that commitment after the events of 9/11. Struggling in the aftermath, I taped the basement windows and stocked the cabinets with nonperishables. And, as recommended, I prepared the four of us and our two dogs for what many of us still feel is inevitable—the bomb to drop on Washington, DC.

After a while, the plastic fell off the windows. The kids discovered a new stash of food, and the leeching plastic water bottles had to be tossed. The crisis, however, still needed tending, and I found my way back to the nonprofit world where I could plant seeds for a better future.

Ten years later, I left the American Association of Naturopathic Physicians and its sister association of medical schools. Few understood that I had given the organization what it needed, and it was time for me to let that baby go. I knew in my body that my effectiveness had reached some kind of cusp. I listened and leapt, confident for my future.

My landing spot taught me enormous lessons, and with skills more honed, I was quick to see the organization was not a good fit for me. Again, it was my body that triggered my attention. It was during this time period that I discovered my five symptoms and my ability to fend them off. The ability to gracefully exit my job required me to use every practice in my toolbox. My welfare and that of my family's depended on maintaining calm. There was no room for upset or story in my negotiations.

After that experience, my slightly-bruised and battered self would abandon my commitment to service, creating a story that even nonprofit work was tainted with modern individualism. "Perhaps," I thought, "if the world is so hell-bent on the almighty dollar, I should just go with the flow." I set out to make real money. "After all," I thought cynically, "corporations are people too, and some of them do great work."

Once again, my body knew exactly what I needed before my brain. I agreed to open the doors of the Organic & Natural Health Association almost six years ago. It happened at a conference table in Chicago where I sat with a small group of brilliant, passionate, and disruptive founders, each highly successful in the broad array of interests they represented. They held a collective commitment to serve consumer interests, a lofty goal far exceeding that of almost every trade association I knew.

At the end of the day, there was a buzz in my head. My body felt lighter. My chest opened and my shoulders relaxed. I was hooked. Our mission to align business, consumer, and agricultural practices for the support of a healthy planet and healthy people sings to me. Every day, our work makes a difference and serves the Seven Generations.

I have one more story that illustrates that, in many ways, we are all beginners, no matter how many years we have used these practices. I choose to work as a consultant. It allows me to take on projects outside my daily domain, including writing this book. Not long ago, I agreed to take a prominent role in a publicly-traded start-up company in a space I know nothing about. I had clearly defined my objective. After all these years in the nonprofit space, I would willingly use some of my time to make the magic fortune a piece of my brain believed was owed to me.

My mother used to tell me I could have done anything in life I wanted; I had chosen to do work that made a difference. "Wouldn't it be nice," I thought, "to finally reap the financial benefits of my effort? After all, it's not like I'm abandoning my principles and leaving the work I love at the association."

I declared I could do both.

It was exciting at first. This unexpected turn led to unique conversations and enormous possibilities. Then, I discovered the machinations of money makes for interesting bedfellows and desperate interests. I felt stifled, unable to use my gifts or create the world I wanted. And, as a result, I was not very likely to achieve that financial success I had envisioned. I found myself needing to repeat my money-making intention over and over to convince myself I wanted to do this work.

Remember the story about Caleb and his sneezing of words across thousands of miles on the phone? This company was his dream, and he was fighting tooth and nail to make it happen. In the end, not even my genuine desire to support one of my dearest friend's success could sustain me.

The workload was light, yet it exhausted me. There was never anything really wrong. There was also never anything really right, at least for me. My body talked to me about this on a regular basis. Tightening with a phone call. Tossing in bed, losing valuable sleep over things I can no longer remember. I was compensated for my time, yet that seemed irrelevant. I lasted a year. Slap me silly if I ever take any more of my now very limited time on this earth to do any work that does not honor my ancestors or serve my great-grandchildren.

For the most part, I have always relied on myself to create my own happiness. What I lacked was the wisdom of my body to keep me pointed in the right direction—one that valued my desire to contribute and serve. Now, I have these tools to keep me on my chosen path and not allow the interests, beliefs, needs, and stories of others to stop me. And, they are just that—practices. There seems to be no end to the learning, and for that, I am most grateful.

I wish for you to explore these practices for the sake of your life, for the benefit of those you love and those who rely upon you, and for the Seven Generations. Go out and create a world by designing your day with intention. Let's make "being in a mood" a positive happening.

Promise to really listen and ask questions. I've never heard of one cat dying from curiosity. The next time you make a request and the answer is no, see if there is room for negotiation, and hold no rancor if there is not. Live your story well, in tune with the actual phenomena, and ready to reframe your feelings and create opportunity. Slamming doors leaves a lasting scar on our DNA.

These practices are all about listening to your body. Learn your five symptoms because your life may depend on it. Please do not beat yourself up when you repeat that turn of phrase that generates a scowl on your partner's face. Do not be too hard on yourself when you choose upset in the face of a traffic hiccup. Words have enormous power, and upset is a contagion without a vaccine.

Choose to hit your reset button and breathe. Never, ever forget to breathe deeply and often because anything worth doing is worth doing well. Be brave enough to push out of your comfort zone, wise enough to feel the changes you experience in your body, and smart enough to teach these simple practices through your life's work. This is how we change the world.

About The Author

Karen Howard, an advocate at heart, is originally from Springfield, Missouri. She has now lived in Washington, DC, for more than forty years, working as Congressional Committee staff, lobbying for health care issues, and working for various professional and trade associations. Life changed dramatically for Karen in 2001, after 9/11. Her mid-west sensible worldview was deeply shaken. She needed to be more, give more, and live more meaningfully. A new journey began and led her to Tai Sophia, the first accredited acupuncture school in the U.S., and its founder, Bob Duggan.

Karen's pursuit in the school's Applied Healing Arts program was transformative. Bob's last gift was to hone his work into a series of simple practices in an apprentice program. Each practice is centered on understanding that how you feel in your body will impact your thoughts, actions, and health. Bob taught Karen how to breathe and changed her life.

The stories in this book illustrate how the practices can create peace in your body and your world of work and family.

These are practices what enable successful navigation through the disruptions, disagreements, and misunderstandings that can ruin a family holiday dinner, disrupt the success of a project, or prevent us from experiencing the joy of life. They are healing. And they require practice.

Reach out to Karen through the book's website: UpsetIsOptional.com.

Made in United States
Troutdale, OR
10/30/2024